Totally Indian

Quick and Easy Traditional Indian Food Recipes

Sarah Spencer

Copyrights

All rights reserved © Sarah Spencer and The Cookbook Publisher. No part of this publication or the information in it may be quoted from or reproduced in any form by means such as printing, scanning, photocopying, or otherwise without prior written permission of the copyright holder.

Disclaimer and Terms of Use

Effort has been made to ensure that the information in this book is accurate and complete. However, the author and the publisher do not warrant the accuracy of the information, text, and graphics contained within the book due to the rapidly changing nature of science, research, known and unknown facts, and internet. The author and the publisher do not hold any responsibility for errors, omissions, or contrary interpretation of the subject matter herein. This book is presented solely for motivational and informational purposes only.

ISBN: 978-1987407013

Printed in the United States

Contents

Introduction _____ 1

A Special Word on Turmeric _____ 13

Breakfasts Recipes _____ 17

Curry recipes _____ 39

Dal (Lentils) recipes _____ 53

Rice Recipes _____ 63

Vegetable Dishes _____ 83

Pickle Recipes _____ 93

Indian Bean Curry _____ 103

Dessert _____ 113

Recipe Index _____ 123

Also by Sarah Spencer _____ 125

Appendix – Cooking Conversion Charts _____ 127

Introduction

Indian food is exhilarating. It is a mixture of exotic ingredients, scents, spices, and flavors. Some may find this cuisine a bit intimidating but today's adventurous and globally astute generation is now opening up to it. Despite the seductive nature of Indian cuisine, food experts say it has not really taken off as one would expect. Sadly, some think of Indian food only as "spicy vegetarian curry." Perhaps the strong spices are difficult to get used to, or the cost is comparatively higher that other cuisines. Another possible reason is the diversity of dishes involved. India is vast in terms of population and land area, and the culture is equally diverse. Hence, the variations due to geographical location, religion, available resources, language, and traditions offer perhaps a too-dizzying array of dishes to choose from. The names are confusing as well as they, too, vary from region to region.

Indian food is not only vegetarian. Chicken, lamb, and fish are popularly used. But the ingredients are always fresh and varied, and many of them are excellent for the health.

The recipes you'll find here are designed to make the dishes easy to prepare without sacrificing the authenticity of the flavors and textures. This is just the beginning of your journey towards experiencing and indulging in fascinating Indian cuisine!

Indian cuisine is an amalgam of influences. It contains touches from the Persians, the Arabs, the Aryans, the Chinese, the Portuguese, and the British. Food preparation has always been a big deal in Indian families and mothers lovingly and meticulously pass on the recipes and techniques to their children, most especially to their daughters.

Surprisingly, many mainstays in Indian restaurants and all-around favorites are actually not Indian inventions. The curry that we know, for example, is actually a British concoction. The spices are Indian but the proportions have a British twist.

Authentic curry is not exactly the same as the one we're familiar with. It is difficult to pinpoint which is "authentic" in India because each region, each state, each family, and each restaurant has its own curry recipe. Other ingredients have been introduced here and there to make the original dishes more appealing. Americans have added cream to palak paneer (Indian white cheese cooked in spinach) while the British have added a tomato-based gravy to chicken tikka masala. Vindaloo is a Portuguese dish (vinha d'alhos) using Indian spices and potatoes (another American addition). Samosas were originally only vegetarian but now also have Pakistani-inspired versions containing meat.

Common Ingredients in Indian Cuisine

Indian cuisine makes use of a vast number of ingredients. This may be confusing or too overwhelming for some. It is important to start with the basics and build your supplies as you go along. Remember that spices lose their flavor when stored for too long so it's better to stock them in small quantities.

The use of a certain spice is not the only requirement to achieve an Indian touch in your dishes. Indian cuisine involves a "layering" of flavors to achieve the desired result. Each ingredient is cooked in a special way at a certain point in the cooking process to release the desired flavor notes. You will notice this in the recipes.

Many ingredients that were previously considered inauthentic, such as cream and potato, are now being incorporated in dishes. After all, authentic Indian cuisine traditionally allows for resourcefulness and creativity in cooking.

Here are some ingredients commonly used in Indian cooking.

Aniseed/Star Anise (Vilayati Saunf)
Use whole. Has a strong flavor and is commonly used in slow-cooked dishes.

Asafetida/Asafoetida (Hing)
This has a fetid odor (hence its name) and must be kept in a sealed container away from other spices. It is added to oil during cooking and its pungent odor mellows to a pleasant aroma. The resulting flavor it imparts is akin to that of leeks.

Bay Leaves (Tej Patta)
Leaves from the laurel tree. These are added for aroma and to neutralize strong flavors. They are not actually eaten but only used to impart flavor.

Black Pepper/Peppercorns
These originated from India — specifically from Malabar and Western Ghats. The flavor is best when freshly ground.

Black Salt (Sanchal/Kala Namak)
A pinkish-gray salt used in India and South Asia. It contains trace elements other than sodium chloride, giving it a pungent odor. Its sulfur content gives an egg-like flavor to vegetarian dishes.

Cardamom (Elaichi)
Stock up on black, white, and green types. Green is most commonly used. It has a sweetish taste with a touch of eucalyptus. Used in pod form or as a powder.

Carom Seeds (Ajwain)
The "seeds" are actually dried fruit, with a bitter, pungent flavor. Best fried in ghee or dry-roasted to enhance its flavor.

Chaat Masala
A pungent-smelling spice blend made from dried mango powder, cumin, black salt, coriander, dried ginger, salt, black pepper, asafetida, and red pepper. It imparts a sweet-sour pungency. This is usually sprinkled over dishes after cooking.

Cinnamon Stick or Cassia Bark (Chilani)
Usually used in stick form and sometimes in powder form, cassia bark is milder and sometimes referred to as "fake" cinnamon. It has a milder flavor but is more commonly used in India.

Cloves
Used whole, with a flavor similar to anise. Use sparingly as it can impart a very strong, medicine-like flavor. It is also used as a remedy for toothache and is a natural preservative.

Coriander (Dhania)
Probably the most widely used spice in Indian dishes. Used in powder form for convenience, as whole seeds have to be toasted until golden and then ground. It gives a mild citrusy note to curries and pickles.

Cumin Seeds (Jeera)
These are black or white in color and in seed or powder forms. It gives a sweetish-bitter, smoky note. Has a stronger flavor when freshly ground.

Curry Leaves (Kadi Patta/Karapincha/Methi Neem)
Also known as "sweet neem leaves." These are usually added at the beginning of the cooking process along with onions. They have a curry-like flavor with a smoky, citrus touch, and are believed to prevent diabetes.

Dal/Daal
This is are often referred to as lentils. More correctly, it refers to a variety of pulses (including lentils, peas, chickpeas, kidney beans, mung beans, and the like) which are split. These are also understood to be cooked with liquid, as in soup. Some common dal are:
- *masoor* - split red lentil
- *mung* or *moong* - split yellow lentils; also called green gram
- *urad* - black lentil or black gram
- *chana* - split chickpeas or Bengal gram
- *toor* - pigeon pea or tropical green pea

Dried Mango Powder (Amchur/Amchoor)
Made from unripe or green mango. The mango is dried and ground into a powder which is used as a souring agent in dishes.

Dry red chilies/Chili Flakes/Chili Powder
Some recipes call for whole or coarsely ground. These chilies range in color from orange to fiery red. Indian chili powder is more pungent than American chili powders, so some adjustments may be needed in making substitutions.

Fenugreek Seeds (Kasuri Methi)
These are used whole and give curry its characteristic flavor.

Fish Masala (Meen Masala)
A special spice mix for fish recipes. Consists of dried or toasted and then ground coriander seeds, black pepper, red chilies, turmeric, and curry leaves. Can be bought ready-mixed.

Flours
Indian cooking makes use of many kinds of flours. Here are some more commonly used:

Aata or *atta* - Finely ground whole wheat flour used to make chapatis, parathas, and other Indian breads.

Gram or *besan* - A gluten-free flour made from ground chickpeas. Used for making pakoras, khandvi, and halwa.

Maida - All-purpose flour used for naan, cakes, and pastries.

Rice flour or *chawal ka atta* - Ground rice used for roti, bhajji, and bhakri. Gluten-free.

Garam Masala
This may be referred to as the authentic curry powder. It is a mixture that basically contains cumin, coriander, cloves, cardamom, cinnamon, and black pepper. Other variations may also contain fennel, mustard, mace, bay leaf, turmeric, nutmeg, and chilies. *Garam* means hot and *masala* means spices. This can be bought ready-mixed at the grocery store. There is no standard formula – proportions vary from home to home, chef to chef, state to state, or region to region.

Ghee
Clarified butter that has been simmered in such a way that the milk solids have caramelized and a nutty flavor is imparted. Used for a variety of dishes or as a substitute for oil.

Ginger
Used as a paste or in powder form.

Green chilies
Green Thai chilies are the usual option, and they must be fresh, so buy only when needed. Serrano may be used for less heat. Jalapenos are rarely used.

Green Chili (Hari Mirch) Paste
A fiery paste of green chilies with lime and salt.

Kashmiri Red Chili Powder (Kashmiri Mirch)
This is a chili powder that is used to impart a rich color with milder heat compared to red chili powder.

Madras Curry Paste
Consists of *garam masala* with additional ingredients such as garlic, ginger, vinegar, and oil. Madras curry is said to be the fieriest of them all. Can be bought ready-mixed at Asian and Indian stores.

Mustard seeds
These are used whole and are yellow, black, or brown. Crush in oil to release its nutty, slightly smoky flavor.

Oil
Mustard oil is a staple but you may also use any vegetable or cooking oil. Ghee is also a popular substitute. Southern parts of India use light sesame oil, which has a high smoking point compared to dark sesame oil (which is more popular in East Asia) and is ideal for deep frying.

Onion Seeds (Nigella/Kalonji)
Black onion seeds are used to enhance the flavor of vegetable dishes. These are first fried in hot oil (cold oil makes it bitter) or are toasted.

Paneer
Traditional Indian unsalted cheese made from fresh milk curdled with lemon juice or vinegar. Cottage cheese is an acceptable substitute.

Red Chili Powder (Lal Mirchi)
Indispensable in Indian cuisine. Made from dried red chilies ground into a fine powder. Adds considerable heat and a little color to dishes. Stores usually sell regular and extra-hot versions.

Rice
Basmati rice is traditional but cooking it may be a bit complex for the beginner or if one is pressed for time. If you're not confident about your rice-cooking skills, you can use parboiled or converted rice (like Uncle Ben's). *Gobindobhog* is a sticky rice popular in Southern Indian recipes and desserts. Jasmine rice can be substituted because it has a good fragrance and flavor.

Saffron (Kesar)
This is expensive and used sparingly. It is dissolved in water, broth, or milk to release its deep golden yellow color to dishes. It may also be toasted and made into a powder.

Tamarind
Blocks of pulp from the sour fruit are used. You take some pieces from the block and soak them in hot water to make them malleable. Break them up and strain them to remove the seeds and skin. The liquid is used as a souring agent.

Tandoori Masala
A spice mix specifically for dishes cooked in the tandoor or traditional clay oven. Consists of *garam masala* with other ingredients like onion, garlic, ginger, and cayenne.

Turmeric (Haldi)
It has an earthy flavor, somewhat bitter and lends a golden yellow color to dishes (it stains wooden utensils and clothes, too). Turmeric was used in ancient times, when the refrigerator had not been invented yet, as a natural preservative. Please also see the special section on turmeric.

Tools and Equipment

One might assume that, because of the exotic blend of spices and the novelty of Indian dishes, highly specialized and expensive equipment might be needed. There is nothing further from the truth. Anyone with a kitchen equipped with the basics will happily find it easy to prepare Indian dishes. In special cases, a little resourcefulness and innovation is all you need.

Take a look at this list of things you will most probably need:

Blender
Some recipes require this to make pastes and purees. It's more convenient than the traditional method using a mortar and pestle.

Chopping boards
Have separate ones for meat and vegetables. Wood or plastic is good.

Colander/Sieve
A great helper for draining rice, vegetables, noodles, and other ingredients.
Cooking spoons

Wooden or metal spatulas, ladles, and slotted spoons will come in very useful. It may be worthwhile to keep separate wooden spoons just for cooking Indian food as the spices can stain and leave residual flavors.

Food processor
Very useful for making purees and pastes. As the flavor of spices remain even after washing, the use of a spice grinder is sometimes recommended.

Grater
Very useful as many recipes require coarse pastes or purees.

Knives
Have at least three different sizes and keep them sharp.

Mixing bowls
Have bowls of various sizes on hand for assembling and combining ingredients. This will help you keep your work flow smooth and organized.

Mortar and pestle
Traditionally, garlic, fresh herbs, and spices are crushed or ground using this. Can also be used to make coarse pastes.

Pots and pans
You must have pans of different sizes for different uses — saucepans, frying pans, flat-bottomed pans, pancake pans, griddles, etc. Heavy-bottomed as well as nonstick are preferable.

Pressure cooker
For Indian dishes that require cooking in their own juices and to speed up cooking time.

Rice cooker and Steamer
Save time and trouble in cooking rice. The steamer attachment will make it possible to steam vegetables while cooking rice.

Rolling pin
This is handy especially for making Indian breads.

Slotted spoon
Useful for fishing out ingredients while simultaneously draining out the liquid or oil.

Spice grinder/Coffee Grinder
Many Indian households make use of a coffee grinder to grind toasted spices. This is the more modern counterpart of the mortar and pestle. Be sure to use a separate one for coffee, unless you like spicy hot coffee!

Spice Box (masala dabba)
This is one item that is not common in non-Indian kitchens. Spices deteriorate easily when not stored properly. Ideally, they should be stored in a cool, dry place, away from direct sunlight. The spice box is the ideal storage container for all your spices. It

is a stainless-steel container with seven compartments, a stainless steel spoon for scooping out the spices, and an airtight lid. This will help make cooking more organized.

Tawa (also called tava)
A flat, disc-shaped, sometimes slightly concave metal pan. Similar to a pancake griddle. This is used for making Indian breads like chapatti, naan, and roti.

Tongs
Another very helpful tool for turning breads or grilled food over. Also good for flipping or picking up fried food.

Wire whisk
This is useful for whisking eggs, sauces, and gravies. Metal is also okay.

Wok
Called kadai or karahi, it can be used for boiling, frying, roasting, pickling, and sautéing.

Now that you've got your basic ingredients and equipment ready, you're all set to cook some homemade Indian dishes!

A Special Word on Turmeric

All recipes in this cookbook make good usage of turmeric, a superfood everyone should add to their diet whenever possible.

Turmeric has been common in Indian and Southeast Asian food preparation for thousands of years and has also been used in medicine. In the West, it seems we are only beginning to take its potential health benefits seriously.

It comes from a root that looks similar to ginger, but its bright yellow/orange color makes it useful for dyes and food coloring, as well.

Turmeric is an excellent source of iron, manganese, vitamin B_6, dietary fiber, copper, and potassium. It also contains several helpful phytonutrients.

Here are the top evidence-based health benefits of turmeric:

1. It is a natural anti-inflammatory compound

Curcumin is the main active ingredient in turmeric. It has strong anti-inflammatory effects and is a very powerful antioxidant. However, the curcumin content of turmeric is not very high, and it is not easily absorbed into the body. Combining it with black pepper helps boost its effectiveness, and since it dissolves in fat, eating it with an oil helps the compound get into your body.

2. Control Diabetes

Some studies have shown that turmeric helps to prevent and control diabetes by regulating insulin.

3. Lower Your Risk of Heart Disease

Heart disease is one of the biggest health problems in the world. Curcumin may help reverse many steps in the heart disease process. Turmeric supplements have been shown to reduce LDL cholesterol in overweight adults, and to reduce the number of heart attacks suffered by patients after bypass surgery.

4. Turmeric Can Help Prevent Cancer

Cancer is a terrible disease characterized by uncontrolled cell growth.

Researchers are still looking at the effects of turmeric on cancer, but they are very encouraged by some early findings. It looks as though curcumin may be able to reduce tumor size, prevent tumors from acquiring a good blood supply, and maybe even prevent cancer from spreading. These are very exciting possibilities, especially considering that it's a natural substance that is non-toxic to the body, unlike mainstream cancer treatments.

5. Preventing and Treating Alzheimer's Disease

Alzheimer's disease is the most common neurodegenerative disease in the world and one of the most important causes of dementia. Unfortunately, there is no good treatment available for Alzheimer's. Therefore, the focus must be on preventing it.

There seems to be good news on the horizon because it has been shown that curcumin can cross the blood-brain barrier.

It is known that inflammation and oxidative damage play a role in Alzheimer's disease. As we know, curcumin has positive effects in both. Whether curcumin can actually slow the progress of Alzheimer's disease (or reverse it) is now being investigated, but it shows promise.

This is all fantastic news, and what's even better is that we don't need to wait for the science to come in. Talk to your doctor, and pick up a turmeric supplement if you like. Turmeric is very unlikely to do you any harm, and as you can see, it might just do you a lot of good!

If you are interested in supporting our overall health, then read on. We have gathered fifty recipes to help show you how to incorporate turmeric into your meals on a regular basis!

Breakfasts Recipes

Low-Calorie Oats Idli Recipe

These healthy, low-carb *idli* made with oats and grated carrots are ideal for those who are calorie-conscious.

Yields: 4 – Preparation Time: 15 minutes – Cooking Time: 25 minutes

Nutrition facts per serving: calories 72.4, total fat 2 g, carbs 11.9 g, protein 3.2 g, sodium 202.5 mg, sugar 1.7 g

Ingredients
4 cups oats
1 tablespoon oil
1 tablespoon mustard seed
1 tablespoon black grams
1 tablespoon chickpeas
4 teaspoons green chilies, finely chopped

2 cups carrots, grated
¼ cup fresh cilantro, finely chopped
1 tablespoon turmeric powder
Water, as needed
A pinch of Eno fruit salt
2 tablespoons salt
1 cup curd/yogurt (slightly sour)

Preparation
1. In a blender, grind the oats to a fine powder.
2. In a saucepan over medium heat, combine the oil, mustard seed, black grams, and chickpeas. Cook for 5 minutes, or until the chickpeas are golden.
3. Add the chopped chilies, grated carrots, and cilantro. Add the turmeric powder and cool for about a minute.
4. In a bowl, mix the oat powder, Eno fruit salt, salt, and yogurt. Add water, if needed to get a smooth but thick batter. Set aside to rest for 10 minutes.
5. Put this mixture in a greased idli tray and steam for about 10–12 minutes.

Poha (Flattened Rice)

Poha is a famous breakfast from western India. It is easy to cook and packed with nutrients.

Yields: 4 – Preparation Time: 10 minutes – Cooking Time: 20 minutes

Nutrition facts per serving: calories 161, total fat 4.1 g, carbs 5.6 g, protein 0.9 g, sodium 141.5 mg, sugar 0.1 g

Ingredients
2 cups poha (flattened rice)
2 tablespoons vegetable oil
A handful of unsalted peanuts
1 teaspoon mustard seeds
1 teaspoon cumin seeds
5–6 curry leaves
2 green chilies, slit lengthwise (optional)
1 medium onion, finely chopped
A pinch of turmeric

1 large potato, sliced very thin
Half a lime (juiced)
Salt to taste
Garnish: chopped cilantro

Preparation

1. Put the poha (flattened rice) in a sieve and wash it under running water for 2 minutes. Set it aside to drain.
2. Heat the oil in a pan over medium heat and add the peanuts. Fry them until they begin to brown. Set them aside.
3. To the same pan, add the mustard seeds, cumin seeds, curry leaves and green chilies. Sauté for 30 seconds, and then add the onion. Fry until it is smooth and translucent.
4. Add the turmeric, and mix. Sauté for two minutes, then add the potato. Stirring often, cook for 2–3 minutes.
5. Add the poha and cook for another minute. Turn off the heat. Pour the lime juice over the poha and mix well.
6. Garnish with chopped cilantro and serve hot.

Upma Recipe

Upma is one of the most common breakfast items all over India. It is quick to prepare using common ingredients, and you can also make it healthier by adding a lot of vegetables.

Yields: 4 – Preparation Time: 20 minutes – Cooking Time: 25 minutes

Nutrition facts per serving: calories 278, total fat 5.1 g, carbs 14.6 g, protein 8 g, sodium 14211.5 mg, sugar 1.1 g

Ingredients
2 tablespoons oil
½ teaspoon mustard seeds
1-inch piece of ginger
15–20 curry leaves
2 teaspoons black grams, skinless
1 medium onion, diced
1 teaspoon turmeric
3 cups water

1 ½ cups semolina
3 green chilies
Salt to taste
1 medium carrot, cut into ¼-inch cubes and blanched
6 green beans, cut into ¼-inch cubes and blanched
¼ cup green peas, blanched
Garnish: ¼ cup fresh chopped cilantro and/or shredded coconut

Preparation
1. Heat the oil in a nonstick pan over medium heat. Add the mustard seeds, ginger, curry leaves, and black grams and sauté for 1 minute.
2. Add the onion and fry for 2 minutes. Add the turmeric and cook for an additional minute.
3. Heat 3 cups of water in a saucepan or kettle.
4. When the onion is browned, add the semolina to the same pan and sauté for 2–3 minutes.
5. Add the green chilies and salt, and cook for 1 minute.
6. Add the hot water to the pan and simmer until most of the water is absorbed. Add the carrots, beans, and peas, and mix. Cover and cook for 1–2 minutes, or until the semolina is cooked.
7. Serve hot, garnished with freshly grated coriander leaves and/or coconut.

Methi Ka Thepla

This flavored flatbread recipe from Gujarati cuisine is prepared with fresh fenugreek leaves. Methi ka thepla is typically served for breakfast and lunch with plain yogurt and mango pickle.

Yields: 4 – Preparation Time: 25 minutes – Cooking Time: 15 minutes

Nutrition facts per serving: calories 95, total fat 3.0 g, carbs 15 g, protein 2.9 g, sodium 30 mg, sugar 0.1 g

Ingredients
1 cup fresh fenugreek leaves, chopped
Salt to taste
1 tablespoon ginger-green chili paste
1 teaspoon carom seeds
½ teaspoon turmeric powder
1 teaspoon red chili powder
1 ½ cups whole wheat flour, plus extra for dusting
1 cup yogurt
1 tablespoon oil

Preparation
1. Put the fenugreek leaves in a bowl. Add salt, ginger-green chili paste, carom seeds, turmeric powder, and chili powder, and mix well.
2. Add the flour and yogurt and mix well. Add a little water and knead the mixture into a hard dough. Add 1 tablespoon of oil and knead again. Cover with a muslin cloth and set aside for 10–15 minutes.
3. Divide the dough into equal portions (a little larger than a golf ball). Flatten and roll them out into thin discs, dusting lightly with flour.
4. Heat a nonstick tawa and roast the theplas, turning and sprinkling with oil until they are golden brown on both sides.

Moong Dal Cheela

Full of fiber and complex carbohydrates, moong dal cheela is an easy-to-make recipe that you can prepare for breakfast.

Yields: 4 – Preparation Time: 4 hours – Cooking Time: 30 minutes

Nutrition facts per serving: calories 98, total fat 4.7 g, carbs 10.1 g, protein 4.5 g, sodium 596 mg, sugar 0.0 g

Ingredients
¼ cup moong dal (split green grams)
1–2 tablespoons water
1 ½-inch piece of ginger, grated
5–6 cloves garlic, roughly chopped
1 medium onion, roughly chopped
3 green chilies, roughly chopped
Salt to taste
¼ teaspoon red chili powder
Oil for shallow frying
¾ cup skimmed milk cottage cheese (paneer)

Preparation
1. Soak the moong dal (split green grams) in one cup of water for 3–4 hours. Drain well, and grind them with a little water, until smooth.
2. Add the ginger, garlic, onions, green chilies, and salt. Add the red chili powder and mix well.
3. Heat a nonstick pan over medium heat and add the oil. Spread a ladle full of batter to a thin disc. Drizzle a little oil on top, and cook on medium heat until the underside is done.
4. Turn it over lightly, sprinkle with some oil, and cook until the other side is also cooked.
5. Serve hot Sprinkle with paneer if desired.

Dhokla

Dhokla is a breakfast from Gujarat. It's delicious! It is a steamed cake made from gram flour, and it has a lovely scent. It's made fresh from scratch with nutritious ingredients.

Yields: 4 – Preparation Time: 5 minutes – Cooking Time: 30 minutes

Nutrition facts per serving: calories 243, total fat 6.1 g, carbs 40.3 g, protein 9.1 g, sodium 1263.6 mg, sugar 0.0 g

Ingredients
2 cups gram flour (besan)
1 cup yogurt, stirred
1 cup warm water (approximately)
Salt to taste
½ teaspoon turmeric powder
1 teaspoon ginger-green chili paste
2 tablespoons oil
1 tablespoon lemon juice

1 teaspoon baking soda
1 teaspoon mustard seeds
2 tablespoons fresh cilantro leaves, chopped
½ cup shredded coconut (optional)

Preparation

1. Place the gram flour in a bowl. Add the yogurt and approximately one cup of warm water and mix until there are no lumps. Add some salt and mix again.
2. Set the mixture aside to ferment for 3–4 hours. When the gram flour mixture has fermented, add the turmeric powder and ginger-green chili paste. Mix.
3. Heat the steamer, and grease a baking pan.
4. In a small bowl, combine the lemon juice, baking soda, and one teaspoon of oil. Quickly add it to the batter and whisk briskly. Pour the batter onto the greased baking pan and place it in the steamer.
5. Cover, and steam for ten minutes, or until the cake is cooked through.
6. Once it has cooled a little, cut it into squares and put it on a serving plate.
7. Heat the remaining oil in a small pan, and add the mustard seeds. When the seeds begin to crackle, remove them and pour them over the dhokla.
8. Serve garnished with chopped cilantro leaves and shredded coconut.

Creamy Spinach Toast

This creamy spinach toast is low in calories, and contains nutrients like calcium and protein to give you a great start to your day.

Yields: 4 – Preparation Time: 20 minutes – Cooking Time: 10 minutes

Nutrition facts per serving: calories 243, total fat 6.1 g, carbs 40.3 g, protein 9.1 g, sodium 1263.6 mg, sugar 0.0 g

Ingredients
2 tablespoons butter
4 garlic cloves, minced
½ onion, diced
½ cup milk
1 ½ tablespoons corn flour
2 cups spinach leaves, finely chopped
Salt, to taste
Whole black peppercorns, crushed, to taste

1 teaspoon turmeric
Red chili flakes, to taste
2 tablespoons heavy cream
¼ cup cheese, grated (more for topping, if desired)
8 slices bread

Preparation

1. Prepare all the ingredients in advance. Place a pan over medium heat and add the butter.
2. Once the butter is melted, add the garlic and sauté until golden brown.
3. Add the onions and sauté for about 2 minutes, or until they are lightly caramelized. Reduce the heat.
4. While continuing to simmer the onions on low heat, mix the milk and corn flour in another bowl.
5. Add the spinach leaves to the onions, and sauté until slightly wilted.
6. Add the mixture of milk and corn flour to the vegetables.
7. Continue to stir and cook for 1 minute, or until the mixture starts to thicken.
8. Add the salt, pepper, turmeric, and chili flakes to taste.
9. Stir for 30 seconds over medium heat, making sure it does not burn.
10. Add the cream and mix well.
11. Once the mixture is thick and creamy, add the grated cheese and mix well.
12. Turn off the heat and allow the mixture to cool.
13. Preheat the oven to 180°F.
14. Spread a spoonful of the mixture over a slice of bread and repeat the process with the other slices.
15. Cover with more cheese, if desired.
16. Place the slices of bread on a baking sheet and bake for 8–10 minutes.

Paneer Paratha

Paneer is the Indian version of cottage cheese. It is highly nutritious, with lots of protein, calcium, vitamin B_2, vitamin B_{12} and phosphorous. Paneer can be a great nutrition-enriched food for vegetarians.

Yields: 4 – Preparation Time: 20 minutes – Cooking Time: 15 minutes

Nutrition facts per serving: calories 243, total fat 6.1 g, carbs 40.3 g, protein 9.1 g, sodium 1263.6 mg, sugar 0.0 g

Ingredients

1 cup whole wheat flour, plus extra for dusting
½ cup all-purpose flour
¼ cup gram flour
Salt to taste
¼ teaspoon turmeric
1 teaspoon red chili powder
¼ teaspoon garam masala powder
½ cup tomato puree
2 tablespoons oil
1 cup cottage cheese
½ cup processed cheese
1 small onion, chopped
½ teaspoon chaat masala
¼ teaspoon carom seeds
Butter for serving

Preparation

1. Put the wheat flour, all-purpose flour, gram flour, salt, turmeric, chili powder, garam masala powder, tomato puree, and oil in a food processor. Gradually add enough water to create a dough, and knead.
2. Mix the cottage cheese and processed cheese in a bowl. Add the onion, chaat masala, and carom seeds, and mix.
3. Heat a nonstick tawa. Divide the dough into equal portions and roll it into balls. Spread each ball in your palm, keeping the edges thinner than the center. Place a small amount of the cheese and onion filling in the middle, collect the edges, and seal. Roll into balls and let them rest for a few minutes.
4. Sprinkle with dry flour and roll up the parathas. Put each paratha on the hot tawa and cook, turning until well cooked on both sides.
5. Serve hot with butter.

Chana Dal Pancakes

Chana dal (split Bengal gram) is great for diabetics because of its low glycemic index.

Yields: 4 – Preparation Time: 20 minutes – Cooking Time: 15 minutes

Nutrition facts per serving: calories 156, total fat 14.1 g, carbs 7 g, protein 1.7 g, sodium 4.9 mg, sugar 0.0 g

Ingredients
½ cup chana dal (split Bengal grams), soaked and drained
½ cup chopped fenugreek leaves
½ cup chopped spinach
½ cup grated carrot
4–6 curry leaves, chopped
1 tablespoon low fat cheese curds, chopped
1 teaspoon grated ginger
1–2 green chilies, chopped
Salt to taste

1 teaspoon turmeric
1 sachet fruit salt
1 teaspoon oil for cooking

Preparation
1. Soak the chana dal (split Bengal grams) and drain well. Mash to make a thick paste, adding some water if necessary.
2. Add the fenugreek leaves, spinach, carrot, curry leaves, cheese curds, ginger, green chilies, and salt. Mix well.
3. Add the turmeric and fruit salt just before making the pancakes and mix well.
4. Divide the mixture into 4 equal portions.
5. Heat a few drops of oil in a nonstick pan, and spread the dough to make a pancake about 5 inches in diameter.
6. Turn, and cook over low heat until golden brown on both sides.
7. Repeat with the remaining dough to make 3 more pancakes.
8. Serve hot.

Misal Pav

One of the most famous of Maharashtrian recipes, misal pav is a scrumptious cocktail of savories and sprouts!

Yields: 4 – Preparation Time: 15 minutes – Cooking Time: 20 minutes

Nutrition facts per serving: calories 298, total fat 17.4 g, carbs 24.7 g, protein 8.7 g, sodium 14.8mg, sugar 0.5 g

Ingredients
For the Misal Masala
1 tablespoon oil
¼ cup onions, thinly sliced
¼ cup grated dry coconut
2 teaspoons coriander seeds
1 teaspoon cumin seeds
3 cloves
3 peppercorns
1-inch stick cinnamon
2 whole dry red chilies
3 garlic cloves

For the Misal
3 tablespoons oil
1 teaspoon cumin seeds
¼ cup onions, finely chopped
1 cup tomatoes, finely chopped
¼ teaspoon turmeric powder
½ cup moong (whole green gram) sprouts
2 ½ cups hot water, divided
Salt to taste
1 ½ teaspoons chili powder
2 tablespoons cilantro, finely chopped

For Serving
½ cup potatoes, boiled
½ cup onions, finely chopped
¼ cup cilantro leaves, finely chopped
8 slices bread
4 lemon wedges

Preparation
1. To make the masala, heat the oil in a large nonstick frying pan over medium heat. Add the onions and coconut and fry them for 2–3 minutes.
2. Add all the other masala ingredients and cook for 3–4 minutes.
3. Remove the skillet from the heat and allow it to cool completely.
4. Once cooled, use a blender to blend to a soft powder (do not add water).

For the misal
1. Heat the oil in a pressure cooker over medium heat and add the cumin.
2. When the seeds break, add the onions and cook for 1–2 minutes.
3. Add the prepared misal masala and fry for 1 minute over medium heat.
4. Add the tomatoes, turmeric powder and a little water (approximately 1 tablespoon). Mix well, and simmer for 2–3 minutes over medium heat, stirring occasionally.
5. Add the sprouts and mix well.
6. Add 2 cups of hot water and salt to taste. Mix well, close the lid of the cooker, and cook for 5 minutes.
7. Let the steam escape before opening the lid.
8. Add the chili powder, ½ cup of water, and cilantro. Mix well and simmer for 3–4 minutes with occasional stirring.

Plating
1. Just before serving, pour the misal into 4 bowls. Sprinkle each with 2 tablespoons of potatoes, 2 tablespoons of onions, and a bit of coriander.
2. Serve immediately with lemon slices.

Curry recipes

Kashmiri Dum Aloo

Dum aloo is a spicy potato curry from Kashmir, a very beautiful but turbulent area. Dum aloo can be made with yogurt or coconut milk.

Yields: 2 – Preparation Time: 15 minutes – Cooking Time: 20 minutes

Nutrition facts per serving: calories 263, total fat 9.9 g, carbs 39.7 g, protein 8 g, sodium 81.2 mg, sugar 7.1 g

Ingredients
10 baby potatoes, peeled
1 tablespoon mustard oil
3 Kashmiri red chilies
1 cup yogurt
1 tablespoon fennel seed (saunf) powder

½ teaspoon ginger powder
¼ teaspoon roasted cumin powder
¼ teaspoon green cardamom powder
¼ teaspoon turmeric powder
Salt to taste
Pinch of asafoetida
Pinch of clove powder
Steamed rice for serving

Preparation

1. Prick the peeled potatoes with a fork and soak them in salty water for 15–20 minutes. Drain.
2. Heat the mustard oil to the smoking point in a skillet over medium heat.
3. Add the potatoes, and fry on medium heat until they are evenly golden brown. Set the whole skillet aside.
4. Grind the Kashmiri chilies with a little water until a smooth paste is formed.
5. Put the yogurt in a bowl. Add the fennel powder, ginger powder, roasted cumin powder, green cardamom powder, turmeric powder, chili paste, and salt. Mix well.
6. Put the skillet back on the heat over medium. Add the yogurt mixture to the potatoes, and the asafoetida, clove powder, and ¼ cup of water. Allow the potatoes to cook in the gravy for 10–15 minutes.
7. Serve hot with steamed rice.

Paneer Butter Masala

Paneer butter masala is a dish from Punjab, in which paneer is cooked in rich, creamy butter and tomato gravy made with tomato puree, onion paste, cashew paste, and some essential Indian spices.

Yields: 2 – Preparation Time: 15 minutes – Cooking Time: 30 minutes

Nutrition facts per serving: calories 389, total fat 26.67 g, carbs 24 g, protein 11.56 g, sodium 906 mg, sugar 20.59 g

Ingredients
2 ½ tablespoons butter, divided
1 teaspoon oil
1 bay leaf
1 clove
One-inch piece of cinnamon stick
1 dried red chili, broken

1 tablespoon coriander seeds, crushed, divided (plus more for garnish, if desired)
1 small onion, sliced
1 teaspoon ginger paste
1 teaspoon garlic paste
½ teaspoon coriander powder
½ teaspoon red chili powder
½ teaspoon turmeric powder
3 medium tomatoes, chopped
1 cup paneer, cut into triangles
Salt to taste
½ cup water
½ teaspoon dried fenugreek leaves, crushed (optional)
1 tablespoon fresh cream

Preparation
1. Heat 1 ½ tablespoons of butter with one teaspoon of oil in a pan over medium heat. Add the bay leaf, clove, cinnamon, red chili, and half of the crushed coriander seeds. Sauté for one minute.
2. Add the onion and stir-fry for 30 seconds, then add the ginger and garlic pastes. Cook for another 30 seconds. Add the coriander powder, red chili powder, turmeric powder, and tomatoes. Cook on high heat until the oil separates on the surface of the masala. Purée the mixture.
3. Heat the remaining butter in a nonstick pan and cook the puréed mixture for two minutes. Add the paneer pieces and salt. Add half a cup of water and cook, covered, on low heat for five minutes.
4. Sprinkle the dried fenugreek leaves and mix in lightly. Remove the pan from the heat and mix in the cream.
5. Serve hot, garnished with remaining crushed coriander seeds.

Potato Curry

In this exotic dish, potatoes are fried and then soaked in a spicy sauce. It's bound to be a favorite!

Yields: 2 – Preparation Time: 30 minutes – Cooking Time: 25 minutes

Nutrition facts per serving: calories 290, total fat 13.9 g, carbs 20.1 g, protein 21 g, sodium 81.7 mg, sugar 3.5 g

Ingredients
½ teaspoon oil
½ teaspoon black grams
4 curry leaves
8 baby onions, peeled
1 medium tomato, roughly chopped
1 tablespoon ginger-garlic paste
Salt to taste
3 medium potatoes, boiled with salt and turmeric powder and peeled
1 sprig fresh cilantro, for garnish

For the paste

4 cloves garlic
1 dried red chili, soaked in hot water
1 teaspoon fennel seeds (saunf)
1 teaspoon cumin seeds

Preparation

1. Make the paste. Put the garlic cloves, dried red chili, fennel seeds, and cumin seeds into a blender. Add a little water, and grind them to a smooth paste.
2. Heat the oil in a deep nonstick pan over medium heat. Add the black grams, curry leaves, and baby onions and sauté for one minute. Add the tomato and stir to combine. Cover and cook for 5–7 minutes.
3. Add the ginger-garlic paste and salt to the pan, together with the ground paste, and mix well. Add 1 cup water and mix well.
4. Roughly mash the potatoes on a plate, and add them to the pan. Simmer until the potatoes are warmed through.
5. Transfer the mixture to a serving bowl and serve hot, garnished with cilantro.

Chicken Tikka Masala

Chicken Tikka Masala is a delicious tomato-based curry that is not too hot. If you like butter chicken, you will like this, too.

Yields: 2 – Preparation Time: 90 minutes – Cooking Time: 45 minutes

Nutrition facts per serving: calories 581, total fat 30.09 g, carbs 48.9 g, protein 36.2 g, sodium 844 mg, sugar 0.0 g

Ingredients

8 pieces boneless chicken
1 teaspoon ginger paste
1 ½ teaspoons garlic paste
1 ½ tablespoons red chili paste
Salt to taste
½ teaspoon black salt
½ teaspoon turmeric powder
1 tablespoon yogurt
½ teaspoon garam masala powder
⅛ teaspoon carom seeds
3 teaspoons lemon juice
½ tablespoon gram flour (besan)
½ teaspoon red chilies, crushed
¼ cup oil, divided
1 medium onion, diced
1 medium green pepper, cut into 1-inch pieces
2 medium tomatoes, seeded and cut into 1-inch pieces
5 garlic cloves, chopped
1 ½-inch piece ginger, chopped
½ teaspoon coriander powder
Pinch of turmeric
½ cup tomato purée
Salt to taste
¼ teaspoon green cardamom powder
½ teaspoon dried fenugreek leaves, powdered
2 tablespoons fresh cream
2 tablespoons honey

Preparation

1. In a bowl, combine the chicken, ginger paste, garlic paste, red chili paste, salt, black salt, turmeric powder, yogurt, garam masala powder, carom seeds, lemon juice, gram flour, and crushed red chilies. Mix well. Let the mixture marinate in the fridge for 1–2 hours.
2. Heat 2 tablespoons of oil in a nonstick pan over medium heat. Add the chicken pieces and cook for 3–4 minutes on high heat. Reduce the heat and continue cooking another 4 minutes, until browned on both sides. Stir in the marinade.
3. Heat the rest of the oil in another nonstick pan, and add the cumin seeds. When they begin to change color, add the diced onions, peppers, and tomatoes, and sauté for 2–3 minutes. Set aside.
4. Add the garlic and ginger to the pan and sauté.
5. Add the coriander powder and a pinch of turmeric powder, and sauté for a minute. Add the tomato puree and mix. Sauté for a few minutes.
6. Add the salt, green cardamom powder, dried fenugreek leaves and mix. Continue cooking until the oil begins to separate. Add chicken pieces with their sauce, and mix.
7. Stir the fresh cream and honey. Add the sautéed vegetables and stir them in.
8. Serve hot with roti or rice.

Chicken Curry

This is a traditional Punjabi chicken curry dish from northern India. Serve with basmati rice or fresh Indian roti, or naan.

Yields: 2 – Preparation Time: 30 minutes – Cooking Time: 20 minutes

Nutrition facts per serving: calories 387, total fat 16.9 g, carbs 26.3.1 g, protein 35.3 g, sodium 1087 mg, sugar 0.0 g

Ingredients
For the chicken marinade
1 tablespoon ginger-garlic paste
1 tablespoon red chili powder, divided
¼ tablespoon turmeric powder
Salt
½ pound chicken, bone in, cut into medium-sized pieces

For the spice paste
½ teaspoon sesame seeds
½ teaspoon cumin seeds
½ teaspoon coriander seeds
3 dry chilies
3 peppercorns
½-inch stick cinnamon
3 cloves garlic
1 tablespoon freshly grated coconut
½ cup water, divided

For the curry
1 tablespoon vegetable oil
2 green chilies, slit lengthwise
2 bay leaves
½ medium onion, finely chopped

White rice, for serving

Preparation
1. Mix the ginger-garlic paste, ½ tablespoon of the chili powder, the turmeric powder, and salt. Rub the mixture on the chicken and set it aside while preparing the spice paste and curry.
2. For the spice paste, heat a cast iron pan until it is smoking over high heat. Lower the heat.
3. Grill all the ingredients EXCEPT for the coconut and water until they release their scent, about 15 seconds, stirring constantly so they do not burn. Set them aside to cool. Blend with the coconut and 3 tablespoons of water until a smooth paste is formed. Set it aside.
4. Heat the oil until shimmering in a heavy-bottomed lidded saucepan over high heat. Turn the heat down. Add the green chilies and bay leaves. Stir until fragrant, about 15 seconds.

5. Add the onion and keep stirring until soft but not brown, about 5 minutes. Add the spice paste and keep stirring until fragrant and until the oil floats on top, about 10 minutes.
6. Add the marinated chicken pieces and stir until they are coated in the spice mix, about 5 minutes.
7. Add the remaining water to thin out the mixture, for more sauce. Season with salt, stir once, and close the lid. Turn the heat to medium. Cook for about 15 minutes, until the chicken is tender. Open the lid, stir, and serve hot with fluffy white rice.

Vegetable Curry

A quick, healthy and comforting dinner after a long day's work. Serve with rice or naan.

Yields: 2 – Preparation Time: 15 minutes – Cooking Time: 15 minutes

Nutrition facts per serving: calories 190, total fat 7.2 g, carbs 30.8 g, protein 3.9 g, sodium 41.6 mg, sugar 6.4 g

Ingredients
2 tablespoons oil
½ teaspoon cumin seeds
2 medium potatoes, cut into small cubes and soaked in water
1 medium carrot, cut into small cubes
Salt to taste
⅛ teaspoon turmeric powder
2 slices brown bread, processed into crumbs

1 tablespoon coriander powder
½ teaspoon red chili powder
1 tablespoon ginger paste
1 cup water
¼ cup green peas
½ cup paneer, cut into small cubes
¼ cup tomato purée
1 tablespoon fresh cilantro, chopped

Preparation
1. Heat the oil in a nonstick pan over medium heat. Add the cumin seeds. When the seeds begin to change color, add the potatoes, carrot, salt, and turmeric powder, and mix well. Cover, and cook.
2. Add the bread crumbs, together with the coriander powder, red chili powder, ginger paste, and water to the vegetables, and mix.
3. Cover and continue to cook for 2–3 minutes or until the vegetables are almost done.
4. Add the green peas, paneer, tomato purée, and bread crumbs and stir to combine. Cover and cook on low heat until all the vegetables are completely done.
5. Garnish with cilantro leaves and serve hot.

Dal (Lentils) recipes

Dal Makhani

Dal makhana has a smooth, creamy texture and a wonderful flavor. This delicacy is a dish from the Punjab region.

Yields: 2 – Preparation Time: 10 hours – Cooking Time: 40 minutes

Nutrition facts per serving: calories 170, total fat 7 g, carbs 20 g, protein 7 g, sodium 670 mg, sugar 0.0 g

Ingredients

¼ cup whole black grams
1 tablespoon dry red kidney beans
Salt to taste
½ teaspoon red chili powder, divided
1 ½ tablespoons butter
½ tablespoon oil
½ teaspoon cumin seeds
½ teaspoon turmeric powder
1-inch piece ginger, chopped
3 cloves garlic, chopped
1 large onion, chopped
2 green chilies, slit
1 medium tomato
½ teaspoon garam masala powder

Preparation

1. Pick, wash, and soak the whole black grams and red kidney beans overnight in three cups of water. Drain.
2. Boil the grams and beans in three cups of water with salt and half the red chili powder (you can add half the ginger too, if you wish) for about 5 minutes in a pressure cooker. Open the lid and see if the red kidney beans are totally soft. If the beans are not ready, close the lid and cook a little longer.
3. Heat the butter and oil in a pan. Add the cumin seeds. When they begin to change color, add the turmeric, ginger, garlic, and onion, and sauté until golden.
4. Add the green chilies and tomatoes and sauté on high heat. Add the remaining red chili powder and sauté until the tomatoes are reduced to a pulp.
5. Add the cooked grams and beans mixture along with the cooking liquor. Add some water if the mixture is too thick. Add the garam masala powder and adjust the salt.
6. Simmer on low heat until the mixture is totally soft and well blended.
7. Serve hot.

Dal Tadka

Dal tadka is a very popular recipe from northern India, and is familiar to everyone.

Yields: 4 – Preparation Time: 30 minutes – Cooking Time: 20 minutes

Nutrition facts per serving: calories 67.7, total fat 1.2 g, carbs 11.11 g, protein 4.1 g, sodium 18.8 mg, sugar 0.1 g

Ingredients
½ cup pigeon peas
2 cups water
2 ½ tablespoons oil
¼ teaspoon mustard seeds
1 red chili, dried
¼ teaspoon asafoetida
½ teaspoon turmeric powder
½ teaspoon red chili powder
½ teaspoon ginger paste

2 cloves garlic, chopped
¼ teaspoon fenugreek seeds
¼ teaspoon cumin seeds
3 curry leaves
2 green chilies, sliced
3 tablespoons onion, minced
2 tomatoes, finely chopped
Salt as required

Preparation
1. Place the pigeon peas in a pressure cooker. Add the water and heat over medium for around 30 minutes, or until they get quite mushy.
2. Reduce the heat to low and continue cooking, stirring occasionally as you prepare the other ingredients.
3. Add the oil to a pan and heat it over medium heat. Once the oil is sufficiently hot, add the mustard seeds and dried red chili. Once the seeds start to splutter, add the asafoetida, turmeric, red chili powder, ginger paste, garlic, fenugreek seeds, cumin seed, curry leaves, green chilies, and chopped onions.
4. Once the onions turn slightly soft, add the chopped tomatoes and fry everything for around 5–6 minutes on medium-low. Once done, add the mushy dal to the mixture. Season with salt to taste, and stir well.
5. Simmer the dal on low heat for 10 minutes, or until the tomatoes become tender, stirring occasionally. After a few minutes, switch off the heat and transfer the dal to a serving bowl.

Chana Dal (Split Chickpeas)

Chana dal (split chickpeas), also known as Bengal gram, is a very common food in India. Yellow chana dal has slightly sweet taste and nutty flavor. It's a very versatile dish, and prepared with different combinations of lentils and vegetables.

Yields: 2 – Preparation Time: 20 minutes – Cooking Time: 15 minutes

Nutrition facts per serving: calories 212, total fat 6.1 g, carbs 29.2 g, protein 11.4 g, sodium 709.9 mg, sugar 0.0 g

Ingredients
¼ cup split Bengal grams (chana dal)
2 teaspoons vegetable oil
1 large onion, finely chopped
½ teaspoon ginger-garlic paste
1 teaspoon red chili powder
1 teaspoon turmeric powder
½ teaspoon coriander powder

Salt to taste
1 large tomato, diced
½ cup water
¼ teaspoon cumin powder
Fresh cilantro leaves, for garnishing

Preparation

1. Rinse the split Bengal grams (chana dal) under cold water. Let soak in cold water for at least 1 hour. Drain and place in a pressure cooker. Cook on high pressure (or if you have the bean/legume setting) for 5 minutes. Let the pressure release naturally, about 10 minutes. Drain remaining water, if any.
2. In the meantime, heat the oil in a nonstick pan over medium heat. Add the onion, and sauté until translucent, about 2 minutes.
3. Add the ginger-garlic paste, red chili powder, turmeric powder, coriander powder, and salt, and sauté for one minute.
4. Add the tomato, cover, and cook until it is soft, about 3-4 minutes.
5. Add the water and drained dal, cover, and cook for two minutes, or until half of the water has evaporated. Add some water if needed. Add the cumin powder and mix well.
6. Serve hot, garnished with cilantro leaves.

Whole Green Gram Dal (Green Gram)

These nutritious green moong lentils are simmered in an onion-tomato broth in your Instant Pot.

Yields: 2 – Preparation Time: 5 minutes – Cooking Time: 25 minutes

Nutrition facts per serving: calories 228, total fat 3.75 g, carbs 37.7 g, protein 13.4 g, sodium 595 mg, sugar 4.5 g

Ingredients

½ tablespoon oil
½ teaspoon cumin seeds
1 green chili pepper, chopped
½ onion medium, diced
¼ tablespoon ginger, minced
¼ tablespoon garlic, minced
1 medium tomato, chopped
⅛ teaspoon turmeric powder
½ teaspoon coriander powder
¼ teaspoon red chili powder
½ teaspoon garam masala
½ teaspoon salt
½ cup whole green gram lentils, rinsed
1 ½ cups water
½ tablespoon lemon juice
Cilantro to garnish
Rice, for serving

Preparation

1. Start the Instant Pot in SAUTÉ mode, and heat the oil. Add the cumin seeds and green chili, and sauté for 30 seconds.
2. Add the onion, ginger, and garlic. Sauté for 1 minute.
3. Add the chopped tomato and spices, and stir.
4. Add the lentils and water. Stir well. Press CANCEL and close the Instant Pot lid with the vent in the sealing position.
5. Press MANUAL or PRESSURE COOK mode and set it for 15 minutes. When the Instant Pot beeps, let the pressure release naturally.
6. Open the lid and add the lime juice and cilantro. Serve hot, with a side of rice.

Mango Dal Recipe

This is an easy dal recipe made with mango and seasoned with cumin seeds, garlic, and onion for a flavorful dal. Mango dal is usually made with green mango, but you have to try this with ripe ones; it adds a little sweet and sour taste to the dal, and it's also a good way of using ripe mangos if they are too sour to enjoy as fruit.

Yields: 2 – Preparation Time: 10 minutes – Cooking Time: 20 minutes

Nutrition facts per serving: calories 186, total fat 4.2 g, carbs 35 g, protein 13.4 g, sodium 591.7 mg, sugar 18.4 g

Ingredients

½ cup pigeon peas
2 cups water, divided
¼ teaspoon turmeric powder
1 cup mango, peeled and chopped
Salt to taste
1 teaspoon oil or ghee
Pinch of asafoetida
½ teaspoon cumin seeds
1 teaspoon garlic, finely chopped
2 green chilies, diced
1 small onion, diced
4 curry leaves
1 tablespoon cilantro leaves, chopped
Steamed rice, for serving

Preparation

1. Soak the pigeon peas for 10–30 minutes.
2. Rinse and cook the pigeon peas in a pressure cooker with 1 cup of water and turmeric powder for about 10 minutes, or until soft.
3. Mash the dal and add 1 cup of water, the mango pieces, and salt. Bring it to a boil, then reduce the heat to low and simmer while preparing the tempering.
4. In a tadka pan or small pan, heat the oil or ghee. Add the asafoetida and cumin seeds, and allow them to splutter. Add the garlic and sauté until light brown.
5. Add the green chili, onion, and curry leaves and cook until the onion becomes light brown.
6. Pour this over the dal and give it a quick mix. Add the cilantro leaves and simmer for 2 minutes.
7. Serve hot or warm with steamed rice.

Rice Recipes

Sabziyon Ki Tehri (Vegetable Rice)

This is a simple recipe for mixed vegetable rice cooked with yogurt, varied spices and cream.

Yields: 2 – Preparation Time: 15 minutes – Cooking Time: 60 minutes

Nutrition facts per serving: calories 286, total fat 3 g, carbs 56 g, protein 8 g, sodium 607 mg, sugar 5 g

Ingredients
½ cup rice
2 cups water, divided
1 medium potato, peeled and diced

1 carrot, peeled and diced
5 green beans, cut on the diagonal
1 cup cauliflower florets
⅓ cup fresh peas or frozen
½ tablespoon mustard oil
1 teaspoon cumin seeds
1 teaspoon garlic paste
¼ cup thick yogurt
1 teaspoon chili powder
½ teaspoon turmeric powder
5 green chilies, sliced
1 ½ teaspoons sliced ginger
½ teaspoon green cardamom powder
½ cup cream
Salt

Preparation

1. Soak the rice in 1 cup of water for 20 minutes.
2. Boil some water in a saucepan. Add salt and blanch the potato, carrot, beans, cauliflower, and peas, separately, for 2–3 minutes before rinsing each in cold water.
3. Heat mustard oil in a skillet. Add the cumin seeds and garlic paste and sauté for one minute.
4. Add 1 cup of water and cook for a minute. Add the vegetables and salt. Simmer for a few minutes.
5. Add the yogurt, red chili powder, and turmeric powder and cook for 5–10 minutes.
6. Add the green chilies, ginger, green cardamom powder, and rice.
7. Gently stir and reduce the heat. Cover and cook until the liquid is absorbed. If the rice dries out, add a little more water.
8. Once the rice is cooked, add the cream and stir to combine. Season with salt, to taste. Serve hot.

Tamarind Rice

Tamarind rice is a dish from southern India, often eaten for lunch or dinner. It is traditionally made using steamed or boiled rice mixed with tamarind paste,
peanuts, coriander, coconut, red chili, curry leaves, jaggery (a kind of unrefined sugar), pepper, mustard
seeds, fenugreek, turmeric, asafetida, and black grams.

Yields: 2 – Preparation Time: 30 minutes – Cooking Time: 30 minutes

Nutrition facts per serving: calories 270, total fat 9.9 g, carbs 36.9 g, protein 9.0 g, sodium 2.2 mg, sugar 0.1 g

Ingredients
1 cup rice, soaked
2 ¼ tablespoons oil, divided
6 whole dry red chilies, broken, divided
½ teaspoon mustard seeds
1 tablespoon split Bengal grams

1 tablespoon split black grams, skinless
½ teaspoon turmeric powder
⅛ teaspoon asafoetida
6 curry leaves
2 tablespoons peanuts, roasted
1-inch piece ginger, finely chopped
1 ½ tablespoons tamarind pulp
Salt to taste

Preparation
1. Rinse and drain the rice, and cook it in 5–6 cups of boiling water. Once the rice is cooked, drain off and excess and water and spread the rice on a plate. Sprinkle it with ¼ tablespoon of oil and mix lightly.
2. Heat the remaining 2 tablespoons of oil in a skillet, and add 4 of the dried red chilies, mustard seeds, split black grams and split Bengal grams. Sauté for 2–3 minutes until the lentils become brown in color.
3. Add the turmeric powder, asafoetida, curry leaves, roasted peanuts, and ginger. Stir-fry for 30 seconds.
4. Add the tamarind pulp and salt and cook for 2–3 minutes.
5. Chop the 2 remaining red chilies coarsely, and stir them in.
6. Add the spice and tamarind mixture to the rice and mix well. Serve hot.

Lemon Rice with Spiced Curd

Lemon rice is a popular South Indian rice recipe where the rice is flavored with lemon juice and is tangy and spicy. The dish is a complete meal in itself, or it can be eaten with curd, raita or any chutney. It is a wonderful way to use leftover rice.

Yields: 2 – Preparation Time: 2 minutes – Cooking Time: 25 minutes

Nutrition facts per serving: calories 300, total fat 20 g, carbs 94 g, protein 14 g, sodium 709 mg, sugar 1 g

Ingredients
2 tablespoons peanuts
4 cashews
1 tablespoon sesame oil
¼ teaspoon mustard seeds
½ teaspoon black lentils
½ teaspoon split chickpeas
1 green chili, split in half

2 dry red chilies
1 sprig curry leaves
Salt to taste
½ teaspoon turmeric powder
1 cup cooked rice
½ tablespoon lemon juice

Preparation
1. Dry roast the peanuts and cashews until slightly browned. Set them aside.
2. Heat the sesame oil in a pan.
3. When the oil is hot, add the mustard seeds, black lentils, and split chickpeas. Cook until the lentils are slightly browned.
4. Add the green chili, dry red chilies, and curry leaves. Cook for 10 seconds.
5. Add the roasted peanuts, cashews, salt, and turmeric powder to the pan. Cook for 10 seconds.
6. Add the cooked rice and lemon juice and mix well.
7. Cook for another 2–3 minutes, until heated through.

Tomato Rice

Tomato Rice is a delicious South Indian rice recipe which is very quick and simple to cook. Make it for breakfast, lunch or dinner; it's good any time.

Yields: 2 – Preparation Time: 25 minutes – Cooking Time: 25 minutes

Nutrition facts per serving: calories 258, total fat 2 g, carbs 53 g, protein 7 g, sodium 68 mg, sugar 5 g

Ingredients
½ teaspoon cumin seeds
1 teaspoon coriander seeds
1 teaspoon poppy seeds
2 dried red chilies, seeded and roughly chopped
1 tablespoon oil
¼ teaspoon asafoetida
1 teaspoon mustard seeds
6 curry leaves

2 medium tomatoes, finely chopped
¼ teaspoon turmeric powder
1 ½ cups cooked rice
Salt to taste

Preparation
1. Heat a nonstick pan, and dry roast the cumin seeds, coriander seeds, and poppy seeds. Transfer them to a dish.
2. In the hot pan, sear the red chilies until fragrant, and transfer them to a separate bowl.
3. Add the oil to the hot pan, together with the asafoetida and mustard seeds. Let the seeds splutter. Add the curry leaves and sauté until they turn crisp.
4. Add the tomatoes and mix well. Cover and cook until the tomatoes turn soft and pulpy.
5. When the dry-roasted ingredients have cooled to room temperature, grind them to a fine powder.
6. Add the turmeric powder and combine. Spoon out 1 ½ tablespoons of the ground powder and add it to the tomato mixture. (You can store the remaining powder in an airtight container.) Mix well and cook for 2 minutes.
7. Add the rice and the chili peppers, switch off the heat, and mix well.
8. Transfer the prepared rice into a serving dish and serve hot.

Bisi Bele Bath

This is a delicious and famous hot lentils and rice dish from Karnataka. It is often confused with other recipes from the region, such as sambar rice and sambar sadam, but they are not the same. This is an authentic recipe that you are sure to enjoy.

Yields: 2 – Preparation Time: 30 minutes – Cooking Time: 30 minutes

Nutrition facts per serving: calories 199, total fat 5 g, carbs 33 g, protein 8.0 g, sodium 922 mg, sugar 7 g

Ingredients
Spice mix (bisi bele bath masala)
2 teaspoons coriander seeds
2 teaspoons split chickpeas
1 teaspoon black lentils
½ teaspoon cumin
¼ teaspoon fenugreek seeds
¼ teaspoon pepper
2 cardamom pods
1-inch cinnamon stick

4 cloves
1 tablespoon dry coconut
1 teaspoon poppy seeds
½ teaspoon sesame seeds
1 teaspoon oil
6 dried red chilies
A few curry leaves
Pinch of asafoetida
Water

Other ingredients
2 tablespoons vegetable oil
3-4 garlic cloves, minced
½ onion, cut into wedges
¼ carrot, chopped
½ potato, cubed
3 green beans, chopped
1 ½ to 2 cups cups water
¼ cup tamarind extract
1 tablespoon peas
1 teaspoon salt
¼ teaspoon jaggery
1 tablespoon clarified butter
1 cup pigeon peas, cooked
2 cups rice, cooked

For tempering
1 tablespoon ghee
1 teaspoon mustard seeds
1 teaspoon fenugreek seeds
⅛ teaspoon turmeric powder
1 dried red chili
Pinch of asafoetida
A few curry leaves
1 tablespoon peanuts, crushed

Preparation

1. Place the spice mix ingredients in a blender. Use a little water to blend them to a smooth paste.
2. Warm the oil in a large and deep sauté pan over medium-high heat. Lightly fry the garlic, about 30 seconds.
3. Add the onion, carrot, green beans, potato, and sauté for about 4-6 minutes, until they begin to change color. Add about 1½ cups of water and the peas. The vegetables should be just covered in water.
4. Add the tamarind, salt, and spice mix paste. Stir a few times to combine all the ingredients. Reduce heat to medium-low, cover and bring to a gentle simmer. Simmer until all the vegetables are tender and cooked through, about 8-10 minutes.
5. Add the jaggery and the cooked rice. Stir gently until well-combined. Continue cooking until rice is warm, about 2-3 minutes. Remove from heat.
6. In a small skillet, heat the ghee. When hot, make a quick tempering by adding the mustard seeds, fenugreek seeds, asafoetida, turmeric powder, red chilies, and curry leaves. Add the peanuts and cover immediately, allowing the aromas to steep for 2-3 minutes.
7. Ladle rice into serving bowls or banana leaves. Top with some of the ghee and spice mixture.

Chicken Dum Biryani

Chicken dum biriyani is one of the most famous biriyani recipes made in India and around the world. The reason it is called dum biriyani is because it is cooked on low heat (dum) to get all the flavors out from the herbs and mix them into the meat and rice.

Yields: 2 – Preparation Time: 30 minutes – Cooking Time: 120 minutes

Nutrition facts per serving: calories 348, total fat 10 g, carbs 48 g, protein 16 g, sodium 804 mg, sugar 2 g

Ingredients
5 strands saffron
½ cup milk
½ cup oil
3 large onions, sliced
1 pound chicken, cut into 1-inch pieces
1 teaspoon ginger paste
1 teaspoon garlic paste

1 teaspoon red chili powder
1 teaspoon turmeric powder
Salt to taste
1 cup fresh mint leaves, divided
1 cup cilantro leaves, chopped
1 tablespoon lemon juice
3 green chilies, finely chopped
2 cups yogurt
7 cloves
2 bay leaves
4 green cardamom pods
1 stick cinnamon
2 cups basmati rice, uncooked
Ghee, as needed

Preparation
1. Soak the saffron strands in the milk, and set it aside.
2. Heat the oil in a kadai and deep fry the onions until brown. Drain them on paper towel. When they are cool, roughly chop them.
3. Place the chicken pieces in a bowl. Add the ginger paste, garlic paste, red chili powder, turmeric, salt, half of the mint, half of the cilantro, lemon juice, green chilies, the fried onions, the oil in which the onions were fried, and the yogurt to the chicken. Mix well and set it aside in the fridge to marinate for two hours.
4. Heat a nonstick pan. Add the chicken along with its marinade and cook on medium heat until the chicken is tender.
5. Boil water in a deep pan. Add the cloves, bay leaves, cardamom pods, and cinnamon.
6. Add some salt and the rice. Cook until rice is one third done. Drain and spread it on a plate.
7. Put the ghee in a deep, nonstick pan. Spread half of the cooked rice out in it.

8. Spread the cooked chicken evenly on the rice layer. Cover the chicken layer with the remaining rice.
9. Drizzle with the saffron-milk mixture, and he remaining mint and cilantro leaves.
10. Simmer for fifteen to twenty minutes.
11. Serve hot.

Corn Pulao Recipe

This simple rice-based pulao recipe is filled with juicy sweet corn kernels and other veggies. It can be eaten as a side with almost any dish.

Yields: 2 – Preparation Time: 30 minutes – Cooking Time: 25 minutes

Nutrition facts per serving: calories 214, total fat 6 g, carbs 38 g, protein 1 g, sodium 789 mg, sugar 0 g

Ingredients

1 tablespoon oil
3 black peppercorns
2 cloves
1-inch cinnamon stick
2 green cardamom pods
1 tablespoon ginger-garlic paste
1 medium onion, sliced
1 ½ cups basmati rice, soaked for 30 minutes and drained
½ cup corn kernels
1 medium green pepper, diced
Salt to taste
¼ teaspoon turmeric powder
1 green chili, sliced diagonally
Tomato-cucumber raita, to serve

Preparation

1. Heat the oil in a nonstick pan. Add the peppercorns, cloves, cinnamon, green cardamom pods, and ginger-garlic paste. Mix and sauté for 30 seconds.
2. Reduce the heat. Add the onion, and sauté until golden. Add the rice and sauté for 2 minutes.
3. Heat 3 cups of water in a microwave for 1 minute.
4. Add the corn kernels and half the pepper, and mix. Add salt and the turmeric powder and mix well.
5. Increase heat in the pan. Add the hot water mixture, mix, cover, and cook for 7–8 minutes or until the rice is half done.
6. Add the remaining green pepper and green chili, mix, cover and cook for 2 minutes or until the rice is done.
7. Serve hot with tomato-cucumber raita.

Kashmiri Pulao

Traditionally, pulao recipes are spicy and savory, but this recipe delights with its use of several dried fruits and raisins and is sweeter in taste.

Yields: 2 – Preparation Time: 15 minutes – Cooking Time: 25 minutes

Nutrition facts per serving: calories 180, total fat 9 g, carbs 21 g, protein 5 g, sodium 0 mg, sugar 0 g

Ingredients
1 tablespoon ghee
10 cashews, halved
1 ½ tablespoons raisins
8 pistachios
1 teaspoon cumin seeds

1 medium-sized bay leaf
2 cardamom pods
1-inch cinnamon stick
½ teaspoon pepper
½ teaspoon turmeric powder
5 cloves
¼ teaspoon fennel seeds
1 medium onion, thinly sliced
1 green chili, split lengthwise
Salt to taste
1 teaspoon ginger-garlic paste
¼ teaspoon red chili powder
1 cup basmati rice, soaked for 30 minutes and drained
1 ½ cups water
1 tablespoon saffron milk
1 tablespoon cilantro leaves, chopped
Onion-tomato raita, for serving

Preparation
1. Melt the ghee in a pressure cooker. Add the cashews, raisins, and pistachios.
2. Sauté on low heat until they begin to soften. Spoon them into a bowl and set them aside.
3. Add all the spices to the pot and sauté until their scents are released.
4. Add the onion, green chili, salt, and ginger-garlic paste.
5. Sauté until the onions turn slightly golden brown.
6. Add the chili powder, and cook for one minute.
7. Add the soaked basmati rice with 1 ½ cups water, and give a good stir.
8. Add the saffron milk and fried dry fruits, and mix gently.
9. Pressure cook for ten minutes on medium heat.
10. Once the pressure is released, gently fluff the rice.
11. Serve the Kashmiri pulao garnished with cilantro, with onion-tomato raita.

Mango Rice

This is a healthy rice dish, a nice change from many pulaos and biryanis, which call for a generous amount of oil or ghee. The key to this rice dish is mango, which lends it a tangy flavor that is counterbalanced with a fragrant tempering of lentils, chilies, curry leaves, and a good measure of peanuts.

Yields: 2 – Preparation Time: 15 minutes – Cooking Time: 25 minutes

Nutrition facts per serving: calories 180, total fat 9 g, carbs 21 g, protein 5 g, sodium 0 mg, sugar 0 g

Ingredients
3 cups cooked white rice, hot
1 ½ cups grated raw green mango, peeled (use more mango for a tangier flavor)
3 tablespoons roasted peanuts
2 tablespoons roasted cashew pieces
Salt to taste

For tempering
1 ½ tablespoons oil
1 teaspoon mustard seeds
1 tablespoon split chickpeas
1 tablespoon split black grams
3–4 dry red chilies
6–8 green chilies, slit
1 teaspoon grated ginger (optional)
¼ teaspoon asafoetida
¼ teaspoon turmeric powder
15–20 curry leaves

Preparation
1. The tempering: heat the oil in a heavy-bottomed pot and add the mustard seeds. Once they pop, add the split chickpeas and split black grams and let them turn red over medium heat. Add the red chilies, green chilies, grated ginger, asafoetida, turmeric, and curry leaves. Toss them for a few seconds.
2. Add the grated mango and stir-fry it for a few minutes. Add the roasted peanuts and cashew pieces, then turn off heat and set it aside.
3. Spread the cooked white rice on a wide plate, sprinkle with salt and add the tempering. Use clean hands to combine the dish, until the tempering is well blended with the rice. Adjust salt.
4. Serve hot.

Vegetable Dishes

Kadhi Bhindi Recipe (Okra in Yogurt Gravy)

Bhindi kadhi is a yogurt-based curry that is spicy and tangy. Very common in northern India, in this curry the bhindi (okra) is cooked in a wok until soft and yet lightly crisp.

Yields: 2 – Preparation Time: 15 minutes – Cooking Time: 40 minutes

Nutrition facts per serving: calories 212, total fat 17. 9 g, carbs 10.5 g, protein 5.7 g, sodium 68.3 mg, sugar 4.4 g

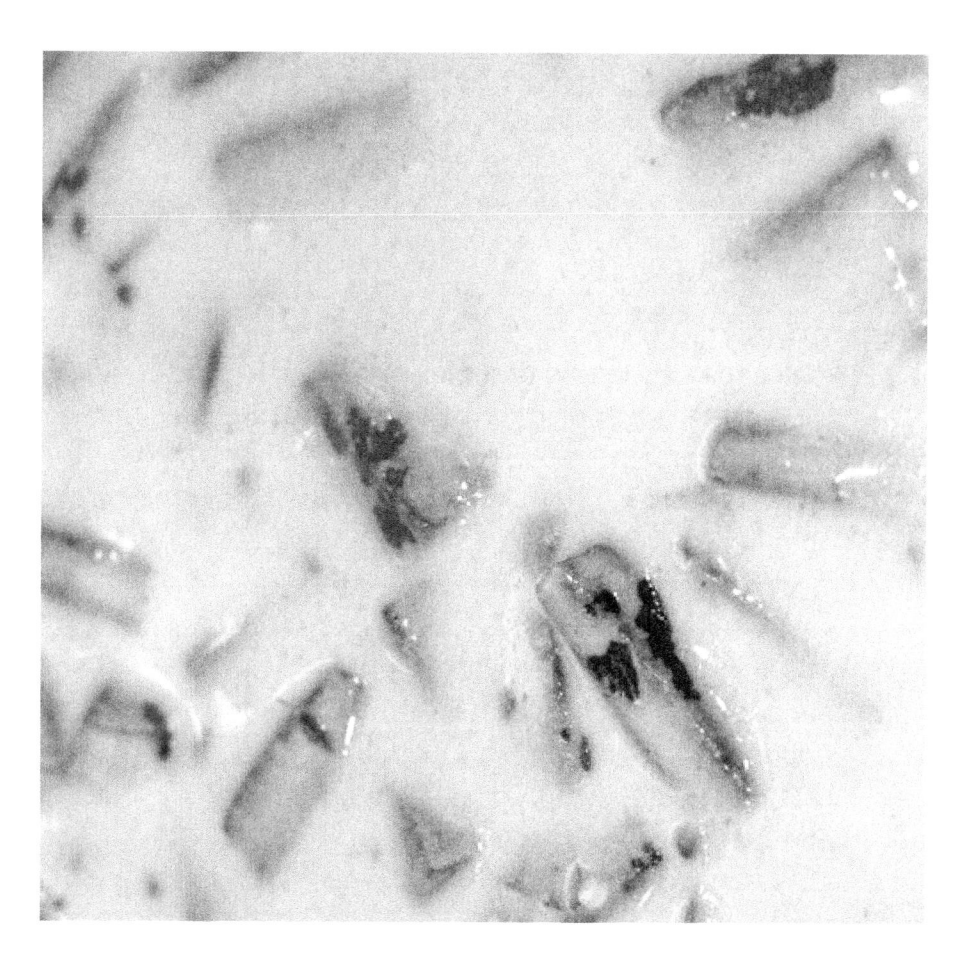

Ingredients

1 cup yogurt
1 ½ tablespoons gram flour
1 teaspoon ginger-garlic paste
1 teaspoon green chili paste
Salt to taste
2 tablespoons water
¼ teaspoon turmeric powder
9 ounces okra
3 tablespoons oil
¼ teaspoon asafoetida
½ teaspoon mustard seeds
1 teaspoon cumin seeds
3 dried red chilies, broken
4 curry leaves
4 black peppercorns
2 cloves
1 tablespoon fresh cilantro leaves, chopped
Rice, for serving

Preparation

1. Whisk the yogurt and gram flour together in a bowl. Add the ginger-garlic paste, green chili paste, and salt, and mix until smooth.
2. Add the water and turmeric powder, stir, and set aside.
3. Trim the tips off the okra.
4. Heat the oil in a deep nonstick pan. Add the asafoetida, mustard seeds, and cumin seeds and sauté until the seeds splutter. Add red chilies, curry leaves, black peppercorns, and cloves. Sauté until fragrant.
5. Add the okra and sauté for 2–3 minutes. Add the yogurt mixture and cook on medium heat until the okra is done and the kadhi has thickened.
6. Garnish with cilantro leaves and serve hot with steamed rice.

Aloo Gobhi (Potatoes and Cauliflower)

This potato and cauliflower dish, aloo gobhi, is packed with flavors.

Yields: 4 – Preparation Time: 15 minutes – Cooking Time 15 minutes

Nutrition facts per serving: calories 91, total fat 0 g, carbs 21 g, protein 3 g, sodium 302 mg, sugar 0 g

Ingredients
4 teaspoons oil, divided
2 medium cauliflowers, cut into small florets
4 medium potatoes, sliced or cubed
1 teaspoon cumin seeds
2 medium onions, chopped
3 teaspoons ginger-garlic paste
4 medium tomatoes, chopped
1 teaspoon turmeric powder
½ teaspoon red chili powder (or to taste)

2 teaspoons coriander powder
¼ cup chopped cilantro (plus more to garnish)
1 teaspoon dry mango powder (amchur)
½ teaspoon garam masala powder
Salt, to taste
Rice and bread for serving

Preparation
1. Heat 2 teaspoons of oil in a pan on medium heat. Add the cauliflower florets and fry for 2–3 minutes.
2. Add the potatoes and fry on medium-low heat for 7–8 minutes, until the potatoes and cauliflower have some brown spots on them.
3. Drain on a paper towel and set aside.
4. In the same pan, heat 1 ½ teaspoons of oil on medium heat. Add the cumin seeds and let them crackle.
5. Add the onions and cook for 2 minutes, until translucent.
6. Add the ginger-garlic paste and cook for another 2 minutes or until the raw smell goes away.
7. Add the chopped tomatoes and cook for 2 minutes until they are a little soft.
8. Add the turmeric powder, red chili powder, coriander powder, and amchur (mango powder).
9. Cover the pan and let the masala cook for 2–3 minutes. Then add the potatoes and cauliflower and mix.
10. Add the chopped coriander leaves and give a good mix.
11. Add the garam masala and cook the potato and cauliflower on medium-low heat for 5–6 minutes.
12. Add some salt, cover the pan, and cook for 6–7 minutes on low heat until the potato and cauliflower are tender but not soggy.
13. Garnish with some more cilantro leaves and serve hot with any Indian bread.

Baigan Ka Bharta (Eggplant Stir-Fry)

Baigan bharta is just one of the several versions of eggplant bharta found in Indian cooking, but many other vegetables can be used. *Bharta* is a dish in which the ingredients are roughly mashed during preparation.

Yields: 4 – Preparation Time: 15 minutes – Cooking Time 15 minutes

Nutrition facts per serving: calories 83, total fat 5 g, carbs 10 g, protein 2 g, sodium 15 mg, sugar 0 g

Ingredients
1 large eggplant
3 tablespoons oil
5 large onions, chopped
3 medium tomatoes, chopped
Salt to taste
1 teaspoon red chili powder
1 teaspoon turmeric powder
2 tablespoons fresh cilantro leaves, chopped

Preparation

1. Roast the eggplant on medium heat until it is cooked and the skin has charred completely.
2. Cool, peel, and mash the eggplant.
3. Heat the oil in a nonstick pan and sauté the onions until they are light golden brown.
4. Add the tomatoes, salt, chili powder and turmeric powder, and sauté until the masala is cooked and the oil rises to the surface.
5. Add the mashed eggplant and mix well. Lower the heat and cook for 4–5 minutes.
6. Add the chopped cilantro and mix well. Serve hot.

Arbi Ki Sabji (Colocasia Roots Fry)

Colocasia is a genus of flowering plants in the family Araceae, native to southeastern Asia and the Indian subcontinent.

Yields: 4 – Preparation Time: 15 minutes – Cooking Time 15 minutes

Nutrition facts per serving: calories 180, total fat 8 g, carbs 24 g, protein 3 g, sodium 160 mg, sugar 0 g

Ingredients
1 pound colocasia (arbi), boiled and peeled
Salt to taste
1 teaspoon turmeric powder
2 tablespoons mustard oil, divided
2 tablespoons cumin seeds
2-inch cinnamon stick
2 tablespoons ginger-garlic paste
2 medium onions, finely chopped
4 green chilies, slit

2 medium tomatoes, finely chopped
1 tablespoon dry mango powder
2 tablespoons coriander powder
1 tablespoon cumin powder
2 tablespoons garam masala powder
2 cups yogurt
2 tablespoons water
Fresh cilantro leaves, finely chopped

Preparation

1. Cut the colocasias into 1-inch pieces and mix with salt and turmeric powder.
2. Heat 1 tablespoon of oil in a nonstick pan. Add the colocasia and cook until light brown in color. Drain the pieces on absorbent paper. To the same pan, add the remaining oil, cumin seeds, cinnamon, and ginger-garlic paste, and sauté for a minute.
3. Add the onions and green chilies and cook until the onions become translucent. Add the tomatoes and cook until soft. Add the dry mango powder, coriander powder, cumin powder, and garam masala powder. Mix well and cook for 2–3 minutes.
4. Add the fried colocasia and mix well. Stir in the yogurt, and lower the heat. Add two tablespoons of water and cook until the sauce thickens.
5. Serve hot, garnished with cilantro leaves.

Paneer Jalfrezi (Cottage Cheese Fry)

Jalfrezi is a rich curry with Indian origins which involves stir frying chopped veggies in oil and spices until thick. The general term jalfrezi means frying meat, fish, or vegetables. This paneer jalfrezi is an easy-to-make medium-spicy curry made with vegetables and paneer.

Yields: 4 – Preparation Time: 15 minutes – Cooking Time 15 minutes

Nutrition facts per serving: calories 449, total fat 19.1 g, carbs 25.3 g, protein 18.8 g, sodium 1212 mg, sugar 2.5 g

Ingredients

2 tablespoons oil
1 teaspoon cumin seeds
2 dried red chilies
1 medium onion, cut into strips
1 medium tomato, cut into strips
½ medium green pepper, cut into strips
1 teaspoon red chili powder
¼ teaspoon turmeric powder
2 green chilies, chopped
1 inch ginger, julienned
1 tablespoon vinegar
½ cup tomato sauce
7 ounces paneer, cut into strips
Salt to taste
½ teaspoon garam masala powder
10 sprigs fresh cilantro

Preparation

1. Heat the oil in a nonstick pan. Add the cumin seeds and red chilies and sauté until the cumin seeds are brown.
2. Add the onion, tomato, and pepper strips to the pan and toss.
3. Add the red chili powder, turmeric powder, green chilies, and ginger. Toss to mix.
4. Stir in the vinegar and tomato sauce. Mix well and cook for a minute.
5. Add the paneer, salt, and garam masala powder and toss to mix.
6. Chop the cilantro sprigs and add. Mix well, and serve hot.

Pickle Recipes

Amla Ka Achar (Gooseberry)

Indian gooseberry pickle, or amla ka achar, is one of the best ways to include this wonder fruit in your diet – it's full of flavor and adds amazing taste to your daily meal. Amla has been used since ancient times in India and is considered a miracle fruit. It is full of vitamin C, vitamin A, dietary fiber and other important nutrients.

Yields: 4 – Preparation Time: 3 hours – Cooking Time 5 minutes

Nutrition facts per serving: calories 102, total fat 7 g, carbs 8 g, protein 1 g, sodium 3306 mg, sugar 0 g

Ingredients

20 amla (Indian gooseberries)
2 tablespoons fennel seeds
2 tablespoon fenugreek seeds
1 teaspoon turmeric powder
1 tablespoon red chili powder
3 tablespoons mustard powder
½ teaspoon asafoetida
½ cup mustard oil
1 tablespoon salt

Preparation

1. In a deep saucepan, cover the amla in water and simmer for about 6 minutes.
2. Drain the amla and allow them to cool.
3. Cut each amla into wedges and discard the seeds.
4. In a mortar, combine the fennel and fenugreek seeds, and crush them.
5. Mix the crushed seeds with the turmeric, chili powder, mustard powder, and asafoetida.
6. In a skillet, heat the mustard oil to the smoking point, and then turn off the heat.
7. Add the spice mixture and the salt; stir well. Add the amlas and toss to combine.
8. Set the mixture aside for at least two hours and store any unused portions in an airtight container.

Aam Ka Achaar (Mango Pickle)

Mango pickle, or aam ka achaar, is a tangy and spicy condiment made from raw mangoes that adds an extra zing to any meal. In India, most households make a whole year's stock of mango pickle in the summer, when raw mangoes are available in abundance.

Yields: 4 – Preparation Time: 3 days – Cooking Time 5 minutes

Nutrition facts per serving: calories 38, total fat 0 g, carbs 10 g, protein 6 g, sodium 1 mg, sugar 0 g

Ingredients

2 ¼ pounds hard green mangoes
⅔ cup salt
4–5 teaspoons red chili powder
2 teaspoons turmeric powder
½ teaspoon asafoetida
3 tablespoons fennel seeds, coarsely ground
2 tablespoons nigella seeds
2 tablespoons dry fenugreek seeds, coarsely ground
3 teaspoons yellow mustard seeds, coarsely ground
2 cloves, coarsely ground
1 cup mustard oil

Preparation

1. Wash the mangoes and let them dry. Wipe them with a clean cloth to make sure no water remains. (Do not peel them.) Cut the raw mangoes into 8–10 medium-sized pieces and remove the seeds. Put the fruit in a large, clean bowl.
2. Add the salt, red chili powder, turmeric powder, and asafoetida. Coarsely grind the fennel seeds, nigella seeds, dry fenugreek seeds, mustard seeds, yellow mustard seeds, and cloves and add them to the mixture.
3. Mix all the dry ingredients in with the mango.
4. Add the mustard oil and mix well using a spatula or spoon. Do not use your hand for mixing!
5. The oil can be added as it is in the pickle. If you want to reduce the flavor of the mustard oil, you can first heat the oil and then let it cool completely before adding. However, this might lead to a slightly viscous pickle.
6. Transfer the mixture to clean, dry jars, and store them in a dry place. Shake the jar once or twice a day for the next 3–4 days. After around 4 days the pickle will reduce and sink to the bottom of the jar. The oil will start floating on the top. If the oil is less and does not cover the pickle completely then you can add 1–2 tablespoons of mustard oil to it.
7. Store the jars at room temperature. The mangoes will become soft in 8–10 days and the pickle will be ready. Refrigerate any unused pickles.

Green Chili Pickle

Green chilies with mustard oil, tamarind, and spices will add a kick to the simplest Indian meal.

Yields: about 4 cups – Preparation Time: 60 minutes – Cooking Time 25 minutes

Nutrition facts per serving: calories 30, total fat 2 g, carbs 2 g, protein 1 g, sodium 800 mg, sugar 1 g

Ingredients
1 pound green chilies, sliced
½ cup salt
3 ounces tamarind
1 cup white vinegar
1 ⅛ cups mustard oil
½ tablespoon red chili powder
½ tablespoon turmeric powder
½ cup fresh ginger, finely minced

8 garlic cloves, finely minced
1 ½ ounces cumin seeds, roasted and ground (about 6 tablespoons ground cumin)
2 ounces large mustard seeds, roasted and ground
½ cup sugar

Preparation
1. Marinate the chilies in salt for at least two hours.
2. Soak the tamarind in the vinegar for at least two hours and extract the pulp.
3. In a large pot, heat the mustard oil and add the red chili powder and turmeric powder. Add the ginger and garlic and mix well.
4. Mix in the cumin and mustard.
5. Pour in the tamarind pulp and mix well.
6. Add the sugar and cook on low heat for 4-6 minutes or until the sugar is dissolved.
7. Add the chilies and cook for 10–15 minutes on low heat until the oil separates. Let cool before placing in jars
8. Serve as a side with your favorite Indian dishes. Store in airtight jars such as Mason jars. They will keep in the refrigerator for up to 4 weeks.

Adrak Ka Achaar (Ginger Pickle)

This ginger pickle is super easy and quick.

Yields: about 4 cups – Preparation Time: 1 hour

Nutrition facts per serving: calories 30, total fat 2 g, carbs 2 g, protein 1 g, sodium 960 mg, sugar 0 g

Ingredients
1 pound raw ginger, julienned
Juice of 13–15 lemons
2–3 teaspoons vinegar
3–4 teaspoons salt, or to taste

Preparation
1. Peel and julienne the ginger.
2. Place the ginger in a large jar. Add the salt, vinegar and lemon juice. Shake the jar vigorously.
3. Let the pickle rest for an hour.
4. When the ginger is a little pink, the pickle is ready to eat.

Nimbu Ka Sada Achaar (Lemon Pickle)

Indian food without pickles is incomplete. Amongst the array of pickles available, this one stands out.

Yields: 4 – Preparation Time: 3 days – Cooking Time 5 minutes

Nutrition facts per serving: calories 45, total fat 5 g, carbs 1 g, protein 0 g, sodium 600 mg, sugar 0 g

Ingredients
2 ¼ pounds sour limes, washed and wiped dry, cut into 4 pieces each
1 ¼ cups salt
1 cup whole red peppers
1 teaspoon asafoetida
1 teaspoon turmeric powder
¼ cup powdered sugar (optional)

Preparation
1. Mix all the ingredients together.
2. Transfer them into a clean jar.
3. Keep the jar in the sun for about a month.
4. Serve.

Indian Bean Curry

Rajma (Indian Red Kidney Bean Curry)

Rajma masala (red kidney bean curry) is a much-loved curry in most Indian households and it goes very well with rice.

Yields: 2 – Preparation Time: 10 hours – Cooking Time 40 minutes

Nutrition facts per serving: calories 135, total fat 0.42 g, carbs 24.52 g, protein 9.01 g, sodium 5 mg, sugar 0.89 g

Ingredients
½ cup red kidney beans
2 tablespoons mustard oil
½ cup onion, finely chopped
1 teaspoon ginger-garlic paste
¾ cup tomatoes, finely chopped
1 ½ tablespoons tomato paste

1 ½ teaspoons coriander powder
½ teaspoon turmeric powder
1 teaspoon red chili powder
¼ teaspoon roasted cumin powder
1 teaspoon dry mango powder
¼ teaspoon garam masala powder
½ cup water
Salt to taste
1 tablespoon fresh cilantro, chopped
Steamed rice, for serving

Preparation

1. Wash the kidney beans and soak them in water for 5–6 hours. Drain well.
2. Place the soaked kidney beans in a pressure cooker with 1 teaspoon of salt and 3 cups of water.
3. Cook until the beans are soft.
4. Remove the pressure cooker from the heat and set it aside.
5. Heat the oil in a pan.
6. When the oil is hot, add the onion and fry until it is translucent.
7. Add the ginger-garlic paste and fry until onion is golden brown.
8. Add the chopped tomato and tomato paste and cook for a minute.
9. Add the coriander powder, turmeric powder, red chili powder, roasted cumin powder, dry mango powder, and garam masala powder, and cook for a few seconds.
10. Add ½ cup water and cook the masala until the oil separates on the side of the pan.
11. Add the cooked kidney beans along with their water, and cook on low heat for 10–15 minutes.
12. Slightly press a few kidney beans with the back of a ladle.
13. Add more water and salt if required.
14. Garnish with fresh coriander.
15. Serve hot with steamed rice.

Chole Masala

This is a spicy chickpea curry prepared with finely chopped onion and tomato. It is usually served with bhatura or puri, but there's no reason you can't try it with roti or parathas too.

Yields: 2 – Preparation Time: 15 minutes – Cooking Time 30 minutes

Nutrition facts per serving: calories 423, total fat 14 g, carbs 60 g, protein 19 g, sodium 100 mg, sugar 14 g

Ingredients
2 tablespoons oil
1 bay leaf
1-inch cinnamon stick
½ teaspoon cumin seeds
1 onion, finely chopped
1 teaspoon ginger-garlic paste
1 tomato, finely chopped
½ tablespoon chili powder

¼ teaspoon turmeric powder
½ teaspoon coriander powder
¼ teaspoon cumin powder
⅜ teaspoon dry mango powder
¼ teaspoon garam masala
Salt to taste
½ cup chickpeas, soaked overnight
2 cups water
½ lemon juice (optional)
1 teaspoon cilantro leaves, finely chopped
Poori, chapathi, or bhatura, or serving

Preparation
1. Heat the oil in a pressure cooker.
2. Sauté the bay leaf, cinnamon stick, and cumin seeds until they turn aromatic.
3. Add the onion and ginger-garlic paste. Sauté until golden brown.
4. Add the tomato, chili powder, turmeric, coriander powder, cumin powder, mango powder, garam masala, and salt. Sauté for a minute.
5. Add the chickpeas and 2 cups of water. Add more water if you want more gravy.
6. Give it a good mix and check the seasonings. The masala water should be slightly salty.
7. Pressure cook for about twenty minutes on medium heat.
8. Allow the pressure to release by itself before opening the cooker.
9. Squeeze in the lemon juice and mix well. Remove the bay leaf, and garnish with cilantro leaves.
10. Serve hot with poori, chapathi, or bhatura.

Black Chana Masala (Black Chickpea Curry)

Chana masala is simple yet rich in its flavors and is infused with aromatic Indian spices.

Yields: 2 – Preparation Time: 15 minutes – Cooking Time 50 minutes

Nutrition facts per serving: calories 101, total fat 3 g, carbs 16 g, protein 5 g, sodium 1400 mg, sugar 2 g

Ingredients

1 tablespoon oil
½ teaspoon asafoetida
1 teaspoon cumin seeds
1 medium tomato, puréed
1 teaspoon salt
1 teaspoon chili powder
1 ½ teaspoons coriander powder
1 teaspoon turmeric powder
2 cups water

1 cup black chickpeas, boiled
1 teaspoon garam masala
1 teaspoon dried fenugreek leaves
½ lemon
1 tablespoon cilantro, finely chopped

Preparation
1. Heat the oil in a pan. Add the asafoetida and cumin seeds once the oil is hot enough.
2. Once the cumin seeds splutter, add the tomato purée and simmer until the oil floats on top.
3. Add the salt, chili powder, coriander powder, and the turmeric powder, and mix everything well.
4. Add water, up to 2 cups, and stir well. Bring it to a boil and simmer for 15–20 minutes
5. Add the boiled black chana and stir well.
6. Add the garam masala and dried fenugreek leaves and stir well.
7. Remove the pot from the heat, squeeze half a lemon over it, and garnish with finely chopped cilantro.

Mixed Bean Curry

This mixed dish is high in protein, fiber, and flavor! The curry is spicy, but you can always adjust the level of spiciness according to your personal taste.

Yields: 2 – Preparation Time: 6 hours – Cooking Time 50 minutes

Nutrition facts per serving: calories 127.9, total fat 4.3 g, carbs 19.1 g, protein 4.8 g, sodium 1400 mg, sugar 2 g

Ingredients
1 cup mixed beans (rajma beans, black eyed beans, dry yellow peas, dry green peas, chickpeas, green moong beans)
Salt to taste
½ teaspoon turmeric powder
1 medium onion, chopped
½ tablespoon ginger paste
1 ½ tablespoons garlic paste
3 tablespoons tomato paste
½ teaspoon red chili powder
1 teaspoon coriander powder
1 cup water
1 teaspoon garam masala
⅛ teaspoon sugar
Rotis or rice, for serving
Fresh cilantro leaves to garnish

For Tempering
2 tablespoons cooking oil
¼ teaspoon cumin seeds
1 cardamom pod
1-inch cinnamon stick
3 whole cloves

Preparation
1. Wash and soak the beans overnight.
2. Boil the dal in 6 cups of water over medium heat with salt and turmeric, until the dal is soft. (This will take much less time in a pressure cooker.)
3. Heat the oil in a heavy-bottomed pan. Add all the tempering ingredients. When the seeds are spluttering, add the chopped onion and fry until golden brown.
4. Add the ginger paste, garlic paste, and tomato paste. Mix well.
5. Add the red chili powder and the coriander powder, and stir until the water evaporates. Add the boiled beans along with more salt, and stir until they are evenly coated with the spices.
6. Add 1 cup of water and bring to a boil. Add the garam masala powder and sugar, and allow the gravy to thicken a little.
7. Remove from heat and serve with rotis or plain rice.
8. Garnish with fresh cilantro leaves.

Green Bean Curry

This is a basic recipe – nutritious, delicious, and rich in protein.

Yields: 2 – Preparation Time: 15 minutes – Cooking Time 15 minutes

Nutrition facts per serving: calories 104, total fat 7 g, carbs 11 g, protein 3 g, sodium 288 mg, sugar 3 g

Ingredients
9 ounces green beans
Oil for deep frying
1 tablespoons oil
1 tablespoon garlic, minced
½ cup onion, chopped
1 tablespoon red chili paste
Salt to taste
½ teaspoon soy sauce
2 tablespoons tomato ketchup
1 teaspoon vinegar

Preparation
1. Cut the beans into long, even pieces.
2. Heat sufficient oil for frying the beans in a kadai.
3. Heat 1 tablespoon of oil in a nonstick wok. Add the garlic and onion and sauté until translucent. Add the red chili paste, salt, and soy sauce, and mix.
4. Add the tomato ketchup and cook on medium heat for 2–3 minutes.
5. Deep fry the beans in the kadai for 3–4 minutes. Drain them, and add them to the sauce. Add the vinegar, mix well, and cook on high heat for a minute. Serve hot.

Dessert

Turmeric Halwa (Pudding)

Haldi ka halwa is quick homemade sweet dish to serve your family and friends. It's full of raw turmeric, which is well known for its health benefits.

Yields: 4 – Preparation Time: 7 minutes – Cooking Time 20 minutes

Nutrition facts per serving: calories 24, total fat 1 g, carbs 4 g, protein 1 g, sodium 0 mg, sugar 0 g

Ingredients
2 teaspoons ginger paste
¼ cup plus 1 tablespoon ghee, divided
10 ½ ounces fresh turmeric, grated
2 cups cream
2 cups milk
¼ pound jaggery

4 teaspoons muskmelon seeds
4 teaspoons dried coconut chips
4 teaspoons almonds
4 teaspoons cashews, chopped
4 teaspoons raisins
4 teaspoons white poppy seeds
1 teaspoon ginger powder
2 tablespoons cashew powder

Garnishing
Rose petals
Cherries

Preparation
1. Sauté the ginger paste in 1 tablespoon of ghee.
2. Add the grated turmeric and sauté for 2 ½–3 minutes.
3. Add the cream and milk.
4. Simmer, stirring occasionally, until the mixture starts releasing the fat.
5. In another pan, combine ¼ cup of ghee and the jaggery. Cook until bubbly.
6. Add this mixture to the turmeric mixture, and stir to combine.
7. Add all the dry fruits, seeds, and powders, and mix well.
8. Serve and garnish with rose petals and cherries.

Turmeric Milk

Turmeric milk is very good for you. It fights inflammation in the body, and may even help with heart disease, depression, and arthritis symptoms.

Yields: 4 – Preparation Time: 5 minutes – Cooking Time 10 minutes

Nutrition facts per serving: calories 100.8, total fat 2.8 g, carbs 20.3 g, protein 1.2 g, sodium 181.1 mg, sugar 16.1 g

Ingredients

¼ cup grated fresh turmeric root OR 1 ½ teaspoons turmeric powder
4 cups milk
4 teaspoons sugar, or as required

Preparation

1. Wash the fresh turmeric roots and pat to dry. Grate them, and set aside.
2. Pour the milk into a broad vessel and bring it to boil.
3. Add the sugar and mix. Add the grated fresh turmeric root or turmeric powder to the boiling milk.
4. Boil on medium heat, stirring once or twice, until the milk turns yellow in color.
5. Strain the milk into a pitcher.
6. Pour it into glasses and serve hot.

Turmeric Laddoo (Balls)

These no-bake turmeric energy bites are gluten free, paleo, high in protein, fiber enriched and anti-inflammatory.

Yields: about 48 – Preparation Time: 5 minutes

Nutrition facts per serving: calories 8, total fat 0.22 g, carbs 1.43 g, protein 0.17 g, sodium 1 mg, sugar 0.07 g

Ingredients
1 pound fresh turmeric roots
4 tablespoons ghee, divided
10 pistachios
5 ounces puffed lotus seeds
1 cup grated coconut

2 ounces walnuts
½ cup watermelon seeds
2 ounces raisins
3 ½ ounces cashews
3 ½ ounces almonds
1 pound jaggery
1 tablespoon ground black pepper

Preparation
1. Peel and grate the raw turmeric. Wear gloves to protect your hands from coloring.
2. Heat about 1 ½ teaspoons of ghee and roast the pistachios, coconut, walnuts, watermelon seeds, raisins, cashews, and almonds until they are slightly crunchy. Take them out and let them cool.
3. When they are cool, coarsely grind them, and set them aside.
4. In a pan, heat a tablespoon of ghee and cook the grated turmeric on medium heat for 10–15 minutes, until the raw flavor goes away and the oil separates. Remove turmeric and set aside.
5. Add jaggery and make syrup. Add the remaining ghee. Continue heating until you achieve a uniform consistency.
6. Remove the pot from the heat. Add the powdered dry nuts to the jaggery syrup. Mix well.
7. Add roasted turmeric to jaggery mix, together with the black pepper. Mix well.
8. Once the mixture is cool enough to handle, make round balls.

Kheer (Rice Pudding)

The pudding is made in many households throughout India, especially on special occasions.

Yields: 4 – Preparation Time: 15 minutes – Cooking Time 45 minutes

Nutrition facts per serving: calories 8, total fat 0.22 g, carbs 1.43 g, protein 0.17 g, sodium 1 mg, sugar 0.07 g

Ingredients
1 cup rice
2 cups whole milk
½ cup sugar
½ teaspoon ground cardamom
½ teaspoon turmeric
1 teaspoon ghee
¼ cup heavy cream
Pinch of salt
Your choice of garnishes: chopped pistachios, slivered almonds, raisins, nutmeg

Preparation
1. Heat the milk over medium-high heat until it boils, and add the rice, sugar, cardamom, and turmeric. Reduce the heat to medium-low, and simmer until the rice is soft and most of the liquid is absorbed. Stir often to prevent sticking.
2. When the liquid is almost all absorbed, add the ghee, heavy cream, and salt. Let it cool slightly to set.
3. Serve warm or cold, garnished to your liking.

Puran Poli (Sweet Lentil Stuffed Flatbread)

Puran poli is a sweet flatbread enjoyed on almost all special occasions in India. Served hot with a dollop of ghee, it is flavorful and filling.

Yields: 2 – Preparation Time: 30 minutes – Cooking Time 20 minutes

Nutrition facts per serving: calories 220, total fat 4 g, carbs 35 g, protein 11 g, sodium 118 mg, sugar 0 g

Ingredients
For the filling
2 cups cooked split Bengal grams
1 cup jaggery, grated
1 tablespoon butter
¼ teaspoon nutmeg powder
½ teaspoon cardamom powder
½ teaspoon fennel powder

For the dough
2 cups whole wheat flour
¼ teaspoon turmeric powder
¼ teaspoon salt
2 tablespoons ghee
Water
Ghee or oil for frying

Preparation
1. Make the dough. Combine the flour, turmeric powder, salt, and ghee in a bowl and mix well using your fingertips.
2. Add a little water and make a soft dough. Cover, and set it aside for 30 minutes.
3. Make the filling. Mix the cooked dal, jaggery, and ghee in a pan and cook until the jaggery is dissolved and mixed in.
4. Simmer the mixture until it starts to leave the sides of the pan and is thickened nicely.
5. Add the nutmeg powder, cardamom powder, and fennel powder, and mix well. Remove the filling from the heat and let it cool.
6. When it is cool, divide both the filling and the dough into 6–8 equal parts.
7. Dust and roll the dough balls out to make 4- or 5-inch circles. Place a filling ball in the center of a dough circle and bring the ends together.
8. Dust the surface and roll it out again again to make a 6-inch circle.
9. Heat a griddle and transfer the stuffed flatbread onto the griddle. Cook on both sides until brown spots appear.
10. Apply ghee on both sides and press the stuffed flat bread using the back of a ladle. Fry until golden brown on both sides.
11. Make the remaining breads in the same manner.

Recipe Index

Breakfasts Recipes _____ 17
   Low-Calorie Oats Idli Recipe _____ 17
   Poha (Flattened Rice) _____ 19
   Upma Recipe _____ 21
   Methi Ka Thepla _____ 23
   Moong Dal Cheela _____ 25
   Dhokla _____ 27
   Creamy Spinach Toast _____ 29
   Paneer Paratha _____ 31
   Chana Dal Pancakes _____ 33
   Misal Pav _____ 35
Curry recipes _____ 39
   Kashmiri Dum Aloo _____ 39
   Paneer Butter Masala _____ 41
   Potato Curry _____ 43
   Chicken Tikka Masala _____ 45
   Chicken Curry _____ 48
   Vegetable Curry _____ 51
Dal (Lentils) recipes _____ 53
   Dal Makhani _____ 53
   Dal Tadka _____ 55
   Chana Dal (Split Chickpeas) _____ 57
   Whole Green Gram Dal (Green Gram) _____ 59
   Mango Dal Recipe _____ 61
Rice Recipes _____ 63
   Sabziyon Ki Tehri (Vegetable Rice) _____ 63
   Tamarind Rice _____ 65
   Lemon Rice with Spiced Curd _____ 67
   Tomato Rice _____ 69
   Bisi Bele Bath _____ 71
   Chicken Dum Biryani _____ 74
   Corn Pulao Recipe _____ 77

Kashmiri Pulao	79
Mango Rice	81
Vegetable Dishes	**83**
Kadhi Bhindi Recipe (Okra in Yogurt Gravy)	83
Aloo Gobhi (Potatoes and Cauliflower)	85
Baigan Ka Bharta (Eggplant Stir-Fry)	87
Arbi Ki Sabji (Colocasia Roots Fry)	89
Paneer Jalfrezi (Cottage Cheese Fry)	91
Pickle Recipes	**93**
Amla Ka Achar (Gooseberry)	93
Aam Ka Achaar (Mango Pickle)	95
Green Chili Pickle	97
Adrak Ka Achaar (Ginger Pickle)	99
Nimbu Ka Sada Achaar (Lemon Pickle)	101
Indian Bean Curry	**103**
Rajma (Indian Red Kidney Bean Curry)	103
Chole Masala	105
Black Chana Masala (Black Chickpea Curry)	107
Mixed Bean Curry	109
Green Bean Curry	111
Dessert	**113**
Turmeric Halwa (Pudding)	113
Turmeric Milk	115
Turmeric Laddoo (Balls)	117
Kheer (Rice Pudding)	119
Puran Poli (Sweet Lentil Stuffed Flatbread)	121

Also by Sarah Spencer

LOUISIANA
COOKING
EASY CAJUN AND CREOLE
RECIPES FROM LOUISIANA
SARAH SPENCER

Best Vegetarian and
Vegan Asian Recipes
from Mama Li's Kitchen
Sarah Spencer

SPICE
IT UP!
THE BEST SPICE MIXING RECIPES FROM
AROUND THE WORLD
SARAH SPENCER

Best Egg Roll, Spring Roll
and Dumpling Recipes
from Mama Li's Kitchen
Sarah Spencer

Best Chinese
Take-Out Recipes
from Mama Li's Kitchen
Sarah Spencer

Best Wok Recipes
From Mama Li's Kitchen
Healthy, Quick and Easy One Pot Meals
For Busy Families
Sarah Spencer

Appendix – Cooking Conversion Charts

1. Measuring Equivalent Chart

Type	Imperial	Imperial	Metric
Weight	1 dry ounce		28g
	1 pound	16 dry ounces	0.45 kg
Volume	1 teaspoon		5 ml
	1 dessert spoon	2 teaspoons	10 ml
	1 tablespoon	3 teaspoons	15 ml
	1 Australian tablespoon	4 teaspoons	20 ml
	1 fluid ounce	2 tablespoons	30 ml
	1 cup	16 tablespoons	240 ml
	1 cup	8 fluid ounces	240 ml
	1 pint	2 cups	470 ml
	1 quart	2 pints	0.95 l
	1 gallon	4 quarts	3.8 l
Length	1 inch		2.54 cm

* Numbers are rounded to the closest equivalent

2. Oven Temperature Equivalent Chart

Fahrenheit (°F)	Celsius (°C)	Gas Mark
220	100	
225	110	1/4
250	120	1/2
275	140	1
300	150	2
325	160	3
350	180	4
375	190	5
400	200	6
425	220	7
450	230	8
475	250	9
500	260	

* Celsius (°C) = T (°F)-32] * 5/9
** Fahrenheit (°F) = T (°C) * 9/5 + 32
*** Numbers are rounded to the closest equivalent

Image Credits

Paneer Parheta
By Akshay Sanjay Agrawal (Own work) [CC BY-SA 4.0 (https://creativecommons.org/licenses/by-sa/4.0)], via Wikimedia Commons

Mango Dal
By Bhaskaranaidu (Own work) [CC BY-SA 4.0 (https://creativecommons.org/licenses/by-sa/4.0)], via Wikimedia Commons

Bisi Bele Bath
By Food and Remedy, LLC - Own work, CC BY-SA 3.0, https://commons.wikimedia.org/w/index.php?curid=31226825

Printed in Great Britain
by Amazon